Four Centuries
of
Scottish Psalmody

THE
PSALMES
of DAVID
in Profe and Meeter.

With their whole Tunes in
foure or mo parts, and
fome Pfalmes in Reports.

Whereunto is added
many godly Prayers, and
an exact Kalendar for
XXV. yeeres to come.

Printed at EDINBURGH by the
Heires of ANDREVV HART,
ANNO DOM. 1635.

TITLE-PAGE OF THE 1635 PSALTER

FOUR CENTURIES OF SCOTTISH PSALMODY

Millar Patrick, D.D.

GEOFFREY CUMBERLEGE
OXFORD UNIVERSITY PRESS
LONDON GLASGOW NEW YORK
1949

Oxford University Press, Amen House, London E.C.4

GLASGOW NEW YORK TORONTO MELBOURNE WELLINGTON
BOMBAY CALCUTTA MADRAS CAPE TOWN

Geoffrey Cumberlege, Publisher to the University

PREFACE

THE Scottish Psalter in Metre begins the fourth century of its use in the Church of Scotland on 1 May 1950. The occasion has been deemed by many to demand that some account of a book which has played no small part in Scottish Church history should be written, for the lack of knowledge about it is widespread.

The General Assembly of the Church of Scotland, on the recommendation of the Chalmers Trust, appointed the present writer to prepare 'a historical survey of Scottish Psalmody', with special reference to the 1650 Psalter. The Church Hymnary Trust had previously encouraged the preparation of a book on the Psalter corresponding to the *Handbook to the Church Hymnary*. And the late Sir Richard Terry, in the preface to his reprint of the music of Dr. Neil Livingston's great monograph on the 1635 Psalter, intimated his intention of leaving an account of the historical setting of that Psalter to be furnished by the writer of these pages.

It became apparent that nothing short of a historical narrative covering the whole history of Scottish Psalmody would answer all these purposes. The writer found that the story of the 1650 Psalter alone would occupy the whole scope of the Chalmers Lectures, as delivered in New College, Edinburgh, and St. Mary's College, St. Andrews. The Lee Lecture on the 1635 Psalter, delivered in the Tercentenary year in St. Giles's Cathedral, Edinburgh, with illustrations sung by the Cathedral Choir, provided the substance of

Chapter 7. The remainder of the present work has been added in order to furnish, so far as existing materials permit, a complete *conspectus* of the history of a book which has for so long occupied a leading place in the worship of the Scottish people, and whose remarkable vicissitudes shed much unexpected light on Scottish life and character.

It has not been thought necessary to multiply musical illustrations, since every good modern hymn-book supplies enough for each period, the Index of Composers and Sources giving the needed guidance. Nor has it been regarded as a requirement in the present book to give historical information about particular tunes, since this may be found in *The Handbook to the Church Hymnary, with Supplement*, and in other books of a similar character.

EDINBURGH

July 1949

ACKNOWLEDGEMENTS

EVERY writer on this subject must own his indebtedness to certain primary authorities: on the French Psalter to O. Douen's classic work on *Clément Marot et le Psautier Huguenot*; on the whole of the Scottish period before 1650 to Dr. Neil Livingston's great edition of the 1635 Scottish Psalter, whose authority is only slightly diminished by the fact that he wrote before the results of Douen's researches were available; and to William Cowan's characteristically faultless *Bibliography of the Book of Common Order, 1556–1644*. The present writer is much indebted also, especially in chapter 9, to Dr. W. P. Rorison's unpublished volume on *The Story of the Scottish Psalter*.

For permission to quote from copyright works mentioned in their several places, and to reproduce illustrations, thanks are due to Mr. Cecil Gray and Messrs. Kegan Paul, Trench, Trübner & Co.; Messrs. Macmillan & Co.; Messrs. Longmans, Green & Co.; Messrs. Adam and Charles Black; Jonathan Cape Limited; Sir William James; Sir John Murray; the Hon. Leslie Runciman and Messrs. Ernest Benn Limited; the Earl of Stair and the Moray Press, Edinburgh; the Cambridge University Press; the Oxford University Press; and the Director of the National Gallery of Scotland.

Individual indebtednesses are gratefully acknowledged to: Miss Anne G. Gilchrist, O.B.E., F.S.A., the nearest surviving relative of Dr. Livingston, and for many years a valued correspondent of the writer; Dr. H. M. Willsher, Dundee; Dr. H. G. Farmer, Glasgow; Prof. G. D. Henderson and Dr. Douglas Simpson, Aberdeen; Dr. Ian J. Simpson, author of a *History of Education in Aberdeenshire*; Mr. W. Beattie, Keeper of the Printed Books, National Library of Scotland, Dr. C. A. Malcolm, Signet Library, and Dr. John Campbell, General Assembly Library—all of Edinburgh; Dr. W. McMillan, Dunfermline; Rev. G. W. Dalgleish, Monymusk; Rev. John Thomson, Carmyllie; Rev. James Thomson, formerly of Martyrs' Church, Paisley; the late Rev. Thomas

Cassels, of Greenock and Dalkeith; and Mrs. John MacRae, granddaughter of T. L. Hately.

The writer has made free use of certain previous writings of his own—in the *Church Service Society Annual* and elsewhere—now all out of print.

To Dr. T. C. L. Pritchard, Glasgow, editor of the music of the 1929 Psalter, a special meed of gratitude is due, for his friendly kindness not only in critically reading the proofs but in giving the writer the benefit of a perusal of his valuable article on the Scottish Psalter written for the new edition, now in preparation, of Grove's *Dictionary of Music and Musicians*.

Miss L. M. D. Patrick, the writer's daughter, compiled the Index.

Finally, the writer is grateful to the Chalmers Trust for nominating him to the General Assembly as Lecturer under the Trust for 1945–8, on the subject of this book; and to the Church Hymnary Trust for its generous interest and a liberal grant towards the cost of publication.

CONTENTS

x   CONTENTS

IV. *The Insufficiencies of the Scottish Psalter*

ILLUSTRATIONS

INTRODUCTION
Why Metrical Psalmody?

THE CHRISTIAN CHURCH, from the beginning, used the Book of Psalms as the basis of its praise. Until the Reformation, prose was the literary medium employed. With the Reformation a breach took place with that immemorial tradition: resort was made, by large sections of the Church, to the use of simple popular verse. The version so produced necessarily became a paraphrase: entirely close and faithful adherence to the original text became impossible. Why, therefore, such a departure from exactitude of translation? Why metrical psalms at all?

For an answer we must cast back a long way in the age which came to a climax in the Reformation. It lies in the fact that the traditional method had doubly proved a failure: alike in words and in music it used a language which the mass of the people could not understand.

For the first three centuries Greek was the language used by the young Church in its worship: not till the middle of the third century did the use of it begin to die out in the West. Latin took its place and became the lingua franca, the medium of spoken communication, of cultivated Europe. Law and letters, diplomacy and the common intercourse of educated men, found it perfect for their purpose. Professors in all the universities lectured in Latin: students conversed and sang their songs in it: there survives a vast body of songs of the wandering students of those days, couched in racy Latin.

Naturally this universal speech of educated people was the language of religion. Only one form of religion was observed in the West. Differences existed between the particular forms observed in different countries, but they were rather in ceremony than in ritual; and by A.D. 1000 the Roman rite had in all essentials superseded every other.

The worship of the Church flowed then, as it still does in the Roman communion, in two distinct and well-marked channels—the Mass and the Quire Offices, with the Missal and the Breviary as their respective manuals; and in both of its forms it drew largely upon the Psalms. In the Mass itself there was no act of importance which had not psalms to accompany it, and the primary intention of the Quire Offices was to provide for the reading or singing of the whole Psalter through, at stated Hours, in the course of every week.

It is true that through this constant religious use Latin had acquired a remarkable flexibility and expressiveness which had not previously belonged to it. But what gain was there in that, when the common unlettered people could only guess its meaning? For a considerable time before the Reformation there had developed a popular hymnody, not officially recognized, but claiming its right of utterance wherever the Church did not forbid, in the everyday speech of the people. The demand became increasingly insistent that Latin should give way to the living language of the

AN EXAMPLE OF SCOTTISH PRE-REFORMATION MUSIC
A page of the Scone *Antiphonarium* (Mid-sixteenth Century)

time, and this 'overwhelming urge for the vernacular'[1]
became one of the irresistible forces which created the
Reformation.

The music also had become an unknown tongue to
the mass of men. It had developed from simple early
beginnings to such a degree that its complexities
baffled any but highly experienced singers. Gradually
the people were edged out from any share in it. So early
as the Council of Laodicaea, held at intervals between
343 and 381, this process of exclusion began, for the
13th canon of this Council embodied this decree: 'Besides the appointed singers, who mount the ambo and
sing from the book, others shall not sing in church.'
This was not immediately enforced, but it indicated
what became a growing tendency. The Quire Offices,
of course, were purely monastic, and none but monks
sang in them; but even in the Mass the singers gradually deprived the people of their part in the responses.

The emergence of plain-song in the sixth century
did much to rectify this wrong. In its first simple form
it was truly popular. Its origin is obscure. Some think
that it derives from the Greek lyric chant, others that
it comes from the cantillation of the Jewish temple.
But other elements appear to combine with these.
All of them were fused together in Byzantium, in the
conflagration of the old civilization, and produced
something entirely new. Doubtless the tradition is well
founded, that it was Gregory the Great who brought
it to Rome on his return, in 595, from his six years'

[1] Winfred Douglas, *Church Music in History and Practice* (Charles Scrib-
ner's Sons, 1937).

office in Byzantium as papal *apocrisarius*, and that he developed the great Roman *schola cantorum*, in which as laboratory, so to speak, the adaptation of the new musical form to the requirements of the liturgy was perfected, before it was made the invariable and obligatory use for the Church's worship.[1]

Plain-song, plain-chant, or Gregorian chant is of the highest musical interest. It is purely melodic, a tune and nothing more. It is entirely vocal: no instrument should accompany it. It has no time measures, no bars: no limit is placed on the freedom it allows: it is meant to be flexible, to fit the words to which it is set, as closely as a glove is fitted to the hand that wears it. Its rhythm is the free rhythm of speech; it is not intended for formal poetry, but for prose.

In its pure form, it is impossible to deny its extraordinary attraction. In the words of Cecil Gray,[2]

'It possesses a purely aesthetic appeal as great as any other form of art that ever existed—an appeal which, however, triumphantly defies all attempts at analysis or definition. Wherein', he asks, 'lies the secret of its irresistible glamour and fascination, of its immemorial power to move us? It seems, on the face of it, to be entirely devoid of every attribute of musical beauty which is commonly deemed essential. It has no determinate rhythm, no harmony or accompaniment of any kind, and its melodic scope is severely limited and circumscribed. Nevertheless, when heard in the appropriate surroundings and under fitting conditions, these simple unisonal chants take on a remote, magical and disembodied quality, a grave ecstasy, radiant yet austere, im-

---

[1] It did not come into universal use for at least a century after Gregory's death, and may not have done so, as Gevaert has shown, much earlier than 900.

[2] *History of Music* (Kegan Paul, Trench, Trübner & Co., 1928), p. 24.

passioned yet serene—and glow as with a secret, inward fire. The voices themselves seem to undergo a curious transmutation and become impersonal, sexless, superhuman almost, giving expression to the inarticulate yearnings and aspirations, not only of the living, but also of the countless generations of the dead and the unborn.'[1]

For Scottish people there is romance in the fact that this was the musical practice of the Church in Scotland for, roughly, 400 years. When the Celtic rite was superseded by the Roman in the twelfth century, plain-song was already in general use throughout western Europe.

By that time, unfortunately, the whole musical movement was away from the first simplicity. Between the twelfth century and the sixteenth an extraordinary advance in musical progress went on. And the field in which all the necessary experimentation took place was the Church, which was the nursing school of the art.

In the tenth century a monk named Hucbald recorded the fact that a revolutionary discovery had been made—that it was possible to sing a tune at two levels, in parallel octaves. By and by the further discovery was made that you can vary the interval: you can do the same thing in fourths and fifths. At a further stage the idea was conceived of making the plain-song tune the *cantus firmus,* and regarding the other tunes which began as parallel to it as not necessarily bound to it, but as free to swing loose from their bondage to

[1] This music may be heard in its purity with the aid of the gramophone records made available by the monks of Solesmes, who after prolonged scientific study of it have restored it to its ancient use.

b

its movement and to follow a movement of their own. Thus you had several independent tunes being sung at the same time. That was how the science, or art, of counterpoint or polyphony began. Its principle was that of singing a number of melodies simultaneously, having their sole unity in the fact that they blended with the *cantus firmus* and with each other in a harmonious synthesis.

This was carried to remarkable lengths. Patrick Hamilton, in his days at St. Leonard's College, St. Andrews, where music was zealously cultivated, composed a work in nine parts and conducted it in the cathedral. One of our great and almost forgotten composers, Robert Carver, canon of Scone, has in an *Antiphonarium* in the National Library of Scotland a Mass in ten parts and a motet in no less than nineteen; the latter constructed, as Sir Henry Hadow attests, on a plan of unprecedented scale and elaboration. And, most extraordinary of all, Thomas Tallis composed a motet in forty parts, written for eight choirs of five voices each, and flowing with an entrancing and majestic richness till it ends, in Sir Henry's words, in 'an ocean of moving and voluminous sound'.[1]

Obviously, as music advanced in this kind of elaboration it had to be written: memory could no longer be trusted to retain and transmit it accurately. And choirs had to be trained to sing it. Thus the Roman example of the *schola cantorum* had to be followed. Song-schools were set up in cathedrals, abbeys, and large towns for

---

[1] W. H. Hadow, *English Music* (English Heritage Series, Longmans, Green & Co., 1931), pp. 3–7.

the training of boys and the singing clergy to bear their parts. Collegiate churches also were constituted and endowed by noblemen, large landowners, and others for the maintenance of Divine Service on a scale of completeness and ceremonial dignity impossible in an ordinary parish church. Chantry chapels also were instituted in these for prayers and masses on behalf of the families of the founders. The collegiate churches were really chantries on a large scale. Each of them had a staff of clergy—a *collegium*; and usually a choir of boys, never large, usually under a dozen, was maintained on the foundation. For these churches were intended to ensure a high standard in the rendering of the music, not only of the Mass, but of the Breviary services at the canonical Hours. In the two centuries between 1342 and 1545 no fewer than thirty-eight collegiate churches were established in Scotland— Trinity College and St. Giles's, Edinburgh among them; Biggar was the last. At all these, the music, which was constantly increasing in elaboration and difficulty, was under constant practice by the choirs of boys and clergy.

Long, however, before the Reformation, extraordinary things took place. The combination of parallel tunes became an exercise intoxicating in its fascination. It was a long time before it was discovered that to combine tunes that would agree with one another was no easy matter. Indeed for a time it was thought that it did not greatly matter although they did not in the least degree harmonize. The consequences were appalling in their discordancy. A time came when chaos

reigned. The singers, carried away by the freedom they
had claimed, ran riot with their experiments; they
cast off all rule, and extemporized the subordinate
parts just as they pleased. Into the Mass itself they
introduced well-known secular melodies, without regard to their first associations. Even the most eminent
composers used such liberties. Over twenty of them
employed the French air *L'Homme armé* as the *cantus
firmus* in the Mass, and the beautiful English melody of
'Western Wynde' was used in the same way. The
results may have been musically entrancing, but worship can have had no place in them.

A contemporary report of the manner of singing in
the twelfth century, by Ailred (or Ethelred) of Rie-
vaulx (1102?–1166), has been preserved to us. He spent
his youth at the Scottish Court as one of the attendants
upon Prince Henry, son of King David, who would
have made him a bishop had he not preferred to be a
monk. He is describing the contortions and extra-
vagances of behaviour of the choristers in his time.

'For what end', he asks, 'is this contraction and dilation of the
voice? One restrains his breath, another breaks his breath, and a
third unaccountably dilates his voice; and sometimes, I am not
ashamed to say, they fall a-quavering like the neighing of horses.
Next, they lay down their manly vigour, and with their voices
endeavour to imitate the softness of a woman. Then by an artificial circumvolution they have a variety of outrunnings. Sometimes you will see them with open mouths and their breath
restrained as if they were expiring and not singing, and by a
ridiculous interruption of their breath they appear as if they were
altogether silent. At other times they look like persons in
agonies of death; then with a variety of gestures they personate

comedians, their lips are contracted, their eyes roll, their shoulders are shaken upwards and downwards; their fingers move and dance to every note. And this ridiculous behaviour is called religion; and when these things are frequently done, then God is said to be most honourably worshipped.'

That was in the early days of the Roman period. As time went on, the state of things did not improve. As the preface to the Book of Common Prayer says, 'There was never anything by the wit of man so well devised, or so sure established, which in continuance of time hath not been corrupted.' The corruptions of Church music became so great that early in the fourteenth century Pope John XXII tried to put down choral singing altogether. Stanford and Forsyth,[1] describing, in terms of the kind of music we are familiar with, what happened when things were at their worst and totally unrelated things were intermixed in the counterpoint used in church, say this:

'When the world turned topsy-turvy, and people first realized that music was not carpentering in 3-inch lengths, a sort of licentious orgy of music set in. It is difficult to explain with reverence just what happened. And if you want a modern analogy with the state of church music at that time, you may imagine one of our composers taking as his base an Anglican chant, and spreading it out so that each note occupied three or four bars; then for his treble using "Take a pair of sparkling eyes" (*allegro molto*), and for his alto part fitting in as much as he could of "Tipperary" or "Onward, Christian soldiers", or both. What the Church service sounded like under these conditions can be better imagined than described. It has been described by contemporary sufferers, and if half of what they say is true, it must have been like rag-time gone mad.'

[1] *History of Music* (Macmillan & Co., 1916), p. 138.

So scandalous became the abuse that the Council of Trent, meeting in 1545–7 to deliberate on how to meet the increasing demands for Church reforms, realizing that some suppressive action was necessary, was disposed for a time to conclude that the only cure for the musical excesses would be to exclude music altogether from the services of the Church. Two things prevented resort to so drastic a remedy.

One was the magnificent use made by certain illustrious musicians of the resources of music in rendering the services of the Church in a manner worshipful in a high degree and artistically far above reproach. Palestrina was the chief among them: in him all the experimentation came to its pure and glorious climax. But others shared in the triumph—the Spaniard Vittoria, Orlando di Lasso in Munich, Byrd and Tallis in England. And with them may be mentioned three Scotsmen some of whose works survived the holocaust of music books at the Reformation—Robert Johnson of Duns, Robert Douglas of Dunkeld, and Robert Carver of Scone. In men like these polyphony rose to the summit of its unapproachable splendour, before the cataclysm of the Reformation rent the world in twain.

The other thing that prevented the Council of Trent from finding the right solvent for the Church's musical problem was its resolute refusal to make any compromise with those who were insistent upon its consenting to the Protestant remedy. At the third meeting of the Council an attempt at compromise was made. The Emperor Ferdinand submitted a scheme of reform which included permission to sing hymns in church in the German vernacular. The French bishops, headed by Cardinal Lorraine, supported this with a plea for a similar concession in favour of hymns in French. But the Papacy would have none of it. Its answer was a resolute refusal to allow the people to praise God in the worship of the Church in their own tongue and in music suitable for them. All attempts to soften this harsh decision were replied to by a policy of repression; and, finally, by the adoption of the weapons of the Inquisition and the Index with which to beat down its opponents, the Papacy 'defied the Christian world'.

The Reformation became an inescapable necessity. And nowhere was the need for it more imperative than in loosening the tongues of the silenced people by restoring to them the right and the power to use their own understandings and voices in the common praise of God. In words and in music new methods to meet their needs had to be found or created; and metrical materials, to suitably simple tunes, furnished the means required.

I

The Pedigree
of the
Scottish
Psalter

Chapter I

The Beginnings of Metrical Psalmody

THE type of public worship developed in the pre-Reformation Church set the issue starkly before those who felt acutely the wrongs that needed to be righted: were the musicians to retain the entire musical part of public worship in their own hands, or were the people to be admitted to a share in it on terms that were practicable for them? Since the Church had restricted its usages to two languages which were not intelligible to most people, two new media had to be found or created by those who were insistent upon reform: on the one hand, words which the people could understand, cast in a form in which they could without undue difficulty read or memorize them; and on the other, music of a type which they would be able to sing.

All the Protestant bodies took the same way of solving both problems: they used versified texts to melodies sufficiently easy to make congregational singing possible.

Inevitably the new methods adopted varied in character and style, so many different factors played their part in determining them—the strength of the reaction against the existing practices, national characteristics and varieties of national inheritance, and, not least, the personal qualities of the leaders of the movements of revolt. These factors produced two distinct developments—one in Germany, the other in France.

Luther was first in the field. Intensely musical as he was, and catholic in spirit, he made it his concern not to make the breach with tradition too extreme. He called the Communion Service which he fashioned 'the German Mass' and retained in the ritual of that supreme act of worship the main elements to which the people had been accustomed. And the new materials he set about preparing for the people to sing he called German psalms: that is, he said, 'spiritual songs, whereby the Word of God may be kept alive among the people by singing'. Moreover, he fell back for his models upon the Latin hymns of the old ecclesiastical order, while he drew also upon the vernacular songs, sacred and secular, which by tradition the people already knew. He used familiar verse-forms, stanzaic in structure, so that a succession of verses might be sung to the same melody. For words, he resorted in a measure to the Psalms, but in the main he used New Testament material, and started the Churches which followed his leadership in the development of Christian hymnody. On the basis thus laid there grew up in due time the vast body of German hymns, which ultimately attained almost immeasurable proportions.

For a time it looked as if Luther's doctrine and policy were going to be adopted by the Scottish people. Lutheranism acquired a strong influence among them, and the first metrical psalms they learned to sing were translations from Luther's German versions into the Scottish vernacular. These came into popular knowledge and use through a book which, next to the Bible itself, did more than any other to further in Scotland the Reformation cause: *Ane Compendious Buik of Godlie Psalms and Spirituall Sangis, collectit furthe of sundrie partes of the Scripture*. It was commonly known as *The Gude and Godlie Ballatis*, and also as 'the Dundee Psalms' and 'the Wedderburn Psalms' because it was produced by three Dundee brothers, Wedderburn by name— James, John, and Robert—all of whom ardently identified themselves with the cause of the Reformation. The eldest fled to France, became a merchant, and died at Dieppe. The second fled to Germany in 1539 or 1540, and at Wittenberg heard Luther and Melanchthon, 'became verie fervent and zealous', and, according to Calderwood, 'translated manie of Luther's dytements into Scotish meeter, and the Psalmes of David. He turned manie bawdie songs and rymes in Godlie rymes.' The third brother was vicar of Dundee.

This collection was published in its first form between 1542 and 1546. Other editions followed, and it is a measure of their popularity that they went on appearing long after the current of the Scottish Reformation had turned into another channel; the last of them was published in 1621. The *Ballatis* never received any kind of ecclesiastical sanction, nor were they sung in the public services of the Church. But Hill Burton[1] is doubtless right in saying that the reason why old copies of the book are so rare is 'not because few copies were printed, but because the book was so popular and so extensively used that the copies of it

[1] *History of Scotland*, vol. iv, p. 352.

were worn out'. The songs were 'long treasured in the hearts of the people and sung in their households'.

Their wide acceptance was partly due to the pungent and searching satire with which, after the manner of the time, they exposed the evils of the Roman system, which had grown so rotten in Scotland that it was toppling to deserved and inevitable ruin. But not least was it due to the fact that the *Ballatis* included twenty-two psalm-versions which enabled the people for the first time to sing in their own homely tongue portions of the Psalter which had until then been doubly barred against their use.

John Knox had every reason to think well of the Wedderburn Psalms. He knew how widely they were known and how powerful an influence they had had in preparing the people for the revolt in which he was to be their chief leader. And he could never forget the incident which he was himself to record in his *History of the Reformation*, how one of these Psalms was the last on George Wishart's lips before his martyrdom. The night before he was apprehended at Ormiston, Wishart 'said "Will ye sing a Psalme?" and so we appointed the 51st Psalme, which was put in Scotishe meter and begane thus:— "Have mercy on me now, good Lord, After thy great mercy" '. These lines are found nowhere but in the Wedderburn Psalms.

Why Knox did not use these Psalms as the basis of a popular Psalter for use in the reformed Church in Scotland is a question for speculation. Possibly the Lutheran doctrine which was given expression in the *Ballatis* made them unacceptable to him.

'Luther was . . . so typical a German that his Church suited
the German people; but for the same reason it could not live
outside Teutonic institutions and the German mind. . . . As a
conservative by nature he professed beliefs that a man of more
consistent intellect would have dismissed, and cherished customs
which a more radical reformer would have surrendered.'[1]

Knox's conception of the reforms the Church needed
was radical indeed, and he may have discerned latent
dangers in the Lutheran system, as he did in the Anglican, which later times were to reveal.

Possibly, on the other hand, the strongly Scots
language used in them may have inclined him against
them. He had lived so long in England that his own
speech was affected to such a degree as to lay him open
to the charge of 'knapping Suddron'—speaking with
an English accent. A version such as the following, of
the 124th Psalm, therefore, cannot have made a strong
appeal to him:

> Except the Lord with vs had stand
>   Say furth, Israell, unfenzeitlie,
> Had not the Lord bene our warrand,
>   Quhen men rais in our contrairie,
> They had us all on liue deuorit,
> With Ire sa scharplie thay vs schorit
>   Sa kendlit was thair crueltie.
>
> For lyke the welterand wallis brym,
>   Thay had ouerquhelmit vs with mycht;
> Lyke burnis that in spait fast rin,
>   Thay had ouerthrawin vs with slycht;
> The bulrand stremis of thair pryde,
> Had peirsit vs throw bak and syde,
>   And reft fra vs our lyfe full rycht.

[1] *The Cambridge Modern History*, vol. ii, p. 343.

Bot louing to the Lord, allone,
    That gaif vs nocht to be thair pray,
To be rent with thair teeth anone,
    Bot hes vs fréd full well thame fray.
Lyke to ane bird taine in ane net,
The quhilk the foular for hir set,
Sa is our lyfe weill win away.

The net is brokin in pecis small
    And we are savit fra thair schame:
Our hope was ay, and ever sall
    Be in the Lord, and in his name,
The quhilk has creat heuin sa hie,
And maid the eird sa mervellouslie,
And all the ferleis of the same.

Any disinclination Knox may have felt to make the
Wedderburn Psalms the exemplar to be followed in the
creation of a Scottish Psalter was likely to be confirmed
when he found that a good alternative was available
in language which, while having the requisite simplicity and suitability for singing by an unlettered people,
was more practicable for his English associates in the
continental beginnings of the Reformed Church.

During the Marian persecutions in England (1553-
8), many English and Scottish exiles fled to the Continent. One influential group of them gathered at
Frankfort. Knox was for a time one of their ministers.
An effort had to be made to harmonize the two forms
of worship represented among them. One party was
immovably attached to Cranmer's policy of a national
Church, with the Book of Common Prayer as its manual
of worship. Knox and those who thought with him
were firm in their belief that a simpler form of prayers

would be 'more meete for their state and time', and that the Church should be constituted on the model Calvin had established in Geneva. Controversy, acute and intricate, ensued, and the Prayer Book party prevailed. They first of all dismissed Knox from the office of preacher, then, using against him certain of his utterances in England, created such political prejudice against him as to subvert his credit with the civic authorities, who expelled him from Frankfort. In March 1555 Knox left for Geneva.

That city was then a republic, governed by its own Council of State. In 1533 it had abolished the Mass. Calvin arrived in 1536, and by his powerful mind and resolute spirit became the chief architect of the Reformed Church. His severe ideas were entirely to the mind of Knox, who accepted the view, among others, that nothing but what was biblical should be used in public worship. This meant that at a stroke the Reformed Church cut itself loose from the entire mass of Latin hymns and from the use of hymnody in general, and adopted the Psalms of the Old Testament as the sole medium of Church praise.

To begin with, the young Church was so preoccupied with doctrine that it made no provision for any offering of praise. Song formed no part of its worship. Its first liturgy, prepared by Farel in 1533, had nothing to say on the subject. It is a singular fact that Zwingli, who was expert in music, hesitated to use it in worship, no doubt because of the injury the excesses of the musicians under the old order had done to the people's worship. Calvin, on the contrary, though himself no musician, was convinced of the necessity of employing it. Like St. Thomas Aquinas before him, his own contemporary Luther, and many Puritan writers after him, he was strongly opposed to the use of instrumental music in church, and even to choral singing, but he strongly favoured 'a simple and pure singing of the divine praises, coming from heart and mouth, and in the vulgar tongue'; and since the people had had no training for such a use of their voices, he held that the best method to adopt would be that of 'selecting children and teaching them to sing in a clear and distinct fashion, so that the people, listening with attention, and following with the heart what was sung by the mouth, might, little by little, become accustomed to sing together' as a congregation. In January 1537 he and Farel, who had been 'the iconoclast of the Swiss Reformation' but was, none the less, a man of progressive mind, drew up together and presented to the Council a scheme for the organization of the Church, in which they recommended the introduction of singing into Divine Service, with the object of infusing into it more warmth and life.

In the following year, however, before anything constructive could be done to give effect to such a design, Calvin was expelled from Geneva. He betook himself to Strasburg, and, finding a small French congregation there, became its minister. During his four years' residence in that city his conviction as to the necessity and value of congregational praise was confirmed and strengthened by what he heard of the singing which had been going on for at least ten years in the strong Lutheran churches around him. And he proceeded, characteristically, to act upon his conviction.

He was not destitute of examples. Some metrical Psalms had appeared in the *Kirchenampt* of 1525, and, according to Zahn, a collection called *Psalmen, Gebet und Kirchenübung* was published in 1526. Calvin's first venture was made in 1539, in a book which was the real fountain-head from which the vast subsequent stream of metrical psalmody began to flow. It consisted of a small volume of four sheets of sixteen pages each, and bore the title: *Aulcuns Pseaulmes et Cantiques / mys en chant. A Strasburg 1539.* It contained seventeen Psalms in metre. Five of them Calvin is believed to have produced himself: Psalms 25, 36, 46, 91, and 138; additional versions of the Song of Simeon and the Ten Commandments are also assigned to Calvin by Bovet and Douen, the two great authorities on the Huguenot Psalter. Psalm 113 and the Credo are given as prose chants. The remaining twelve metrical Psalms—1, 2, 3, 15, 19, 32, 51, 103, 114, 130, 137, and 143—were by Clément Marot, and apparently lay ready to Calvin's hand.

Marot was born at Cahors in Guienne about 1497. His father, Jean Marot, was court-poet and *valet de chambre* to Anne of Brittany, queen of Charles VIII and Louis XII, and young Clément was brought up at Paris in the atmosphere of the Court. In due time he obtained an appointment in the household of the sister of Francis I, the famous Marguerite, Duchess of Alençon and Queen of Navarre. Among his endowments

Clément added to wit a notable poetic gift, and he began early to use both skills with damaging effectiveness in biting satires upon the corruptions of the Roman Church. For one of his pieces, before he was thirty, he suffered imprisonment at the instigation of the Sorbonne, and ever after he was an object of watchful ecclesiastical suspicion. Though gay in spirit and in taste and habit a courtier, he had a sincere sympathy with the Reformed doctrine, even to the point of being prepared, if need were, to die for his belief. When in 1534 persecution of the Protestants broke out in France, he took refuge, with many others—Calvin among them—at the Court of Renée, Duchess of Ferrara, whose sympathies, like those of Marguerite, were with the Reforming party. He was aware that his life was in danger. A poetic epistle written by him at that time to the King, Francis I, shows at once how acute this awareness was, and how ready he was to face the worst consequences. Part of this epistle is translated thus by Professor Henry Morley:

> O Lord my God, this faith in me forgive,
> That for Thy glory Thou hast let me live;
> Then, since it has not pleased Thee to allow
> That my vile flesh pass into ashes now,
> Make me to seek, while yet I write for men,
> Thine honour in the service of my pen;
> And if predestined this my body be,
> One day in flames to die by Thy decree,
> Not for a foolish cause be this, O Lord
> My God, but for Thyself and for Thy Word.
> And may the torture, Father, I entreat,
> Not wring my soul with anguish so complete

> That from its memory the pain should thrust
> Thee in whom only lieth all its trust;
> So that I may, when the long rest draws nigh,
> Call upon Thee with the last breath I sigh.

In 1537 it was possible for Marot to return to Paris and resume his post at the Court of King Francis. Four years previously, in 1533, there had been published *Le Miroir de tres chretienne Princesse Marguerite de France, Royne de Navarre*. At the end of the first part of it appeared *Le vi^e Pseavlme de Dauid, translaté en francoys selon l'hebreu par Clément Marot, valet de chambre du Roy*. Now, in Paris once more, Marot translated and versified other Psalms, and, as each was completed, he presented copies in manuscript to the King and members of the Royal Family. These were received with favour, especially by the Dauphin (afterwards Henry II) who took delight in singing them himself. Soon all the Court was singing them: they became the fashion of the hour. For music, any light tune would serve: they were sung as ballads were, without any religious implication. Each of the courtiers adopted a special Psalm as his own. Thus, for example,

'Henry, as yet without an heir, sang to his own music Psalm CXXVIII, which promises to the God-fearing man a wife "as the fruitful vine" and children "like the olive branches". Catherine de Medicis, then a childless wife, is said to have taken as her favourites Psalm VI ("O Lord, rebuke me not in thine indignation") and Psalm CXLII ("I cried unto the Lord with my voice"). Anthony, King of Navarre, chose Psalm XLIII ("Give sentence with me, O God"). Diane de Poitiers sang the *De Profundis* (Psalm CXXX) to the air *Baisez-moi donc beau sire*. In after years, when Catherine had borne her husband ten children, Henry II carolled Psalm XLII ("Like as the hart desireth the water-brooks") as he hunted the stag in the forest of Fontainebleau, riding by the side of Diane, for the motto of whose portrait as a huntress he chose the first verse of his favourite psalm.'[1]

On New Year's Day, 1540, the Emperor Charles V visited Francis in Paris. Marot took the opportunity to present to him copies of thirty of his psalm-versions, and the Emperor not only expressed his pleasure by a gift of 200 golden doubloons, but requested that a psalm should be composed expressly for himself. Such imperial favour emboldened the author to proceed to publication, and about the beginning of 1542 there appeared *Trente Pseaulmes de Dauid, mis en francoys par Clement Marot, valet de chambre du Roy* (Paris, Roffet).

Prior to publication, copies of these versions appear to have been circulated widely in manuscript. Some of them came thus into Calvin's hands, and twelve were included in the 1539 Strasburg Psalter. Not, however, as the author had written them: they exhibited considerable variations from Marot's text. Douen states his conviction that the alterations must have been made by a Carmelite monk, Pierre Alexandre by name, who was in the service of the Queen of Hungary, and who, without permission, published at Antwerp in 1541 a collection of *Psalmes de Dauid, translatez de plusieurs autheures, et principallement de Cle. Marot. Veu, recongneu et corrigé par les theologiens, nommement par M.F. Pierre Alexandre, concionateur ordinaire de la Royne de Hongrie.* Marot's thirty Psalms, though not yet published, were included, with fifteen by other persons who are either

[1] R. E. Prothero, *The Psalms in Human Life*, Ch. vii, p. 168.

anonymous or indicated only by initials. The manuscript of twelve came into the hands of Calvin, then looking round for materials for his experimental Psalter, and these, with Alexandre's 'improvements', were embodied by Calvin in his book.

The music of the Strasburg Psalter is believed to have been edited by Matthäus Greiter, at one time a monk and singer in the cathedral, who for a time devoted his musical gifts to the service of the Lutheran Church, but before his death recanted and returned to the Roman obedience. Scholars are agreed that his task was one of collection and arrangement only, not of composition. The sources of the tunes cannot be traced, with two exceptions. One (No. 16) was taken from an old French Noël which was current in the sixteenth century. Another (No. 8) is the famous Psalm 36 (68), which became the battle-song of the Huguenots, and was included not only in the French Psalter of 1562, but in the English and Scottish Psalters of 1562 and 1564. Zahn gives its date as 1526. This, and the tune known as Psalm 130 (No. 15), are the only two tunes which have survived from the Strasburg Psalter into modern use. Both will be found in the *Revised Church Hymnary* (217 and 342).

Chapter 2

The French Psalter, 1541–62

CALVIN's exile ended in September 1541, and he returned to Geneva. From that time till his death in 1564, though officially only a pastor and professor, he was virtually ruler of the city-republic. He imposed upon the community an iron rule of discipline in manners and morals.

Two months after his arrival, he was authorized by the Council to introduce the Strasburg Psalms into congregational use. Those by Marot were reprinted in the form which Alexandre had given them, and it was not until Marot, indicted for heresy, sought a refuge in Geneva, that Calvin became aware of the unauthorized alterations. At once he adopted the authentic text; although some of Alexandre's 'improvements' were retained. He dropped the five versions attributed to himself and substituted others with which Marot furnished him; he also invited the poet to make further contributions. The result appeared in August 1543, when Marot published his *Cinquante Pseaulmes*, containing the original thirty in revised form, and twenty new ones (of which the Song of Simeon was counted as one), the Commandments, the Articles of Faith, the Lord's Prayer, the *Magnificat*, and Prayers before and after meat. No music appears to have been published with them.

Pſalme CXXIX.

V fond de ma penſe e Au fōd de to

ennuys Dieu, ie t'ay adreſ ſe e ma clameur iour

τ nuict; Entēds ma voix plāicriue ſeigneur il

eſt ſaiſon, Ton aureil l'en tentiue ſoit a

mon o rai ſon.

PAGE FROM CALVIN'S FIRST PSALTER OF 1539
(See p. 11: '129' is the psalm known to us as 130)

OCTANTENEVF

PSEAVMES DE DA-
VID, MIS EN RIME
FRANCOISE:
A sçauoir,

QVARANTENEVF PAR CLEMENT
Marot, auec le Cantique de Simeon, Les dix Commandemens, & le
Cantique de Moyse. ET,
QVARANTE PAR THEODORE DE
Besze, de Vezelay en Bourgongne.

A TOVS CHRESTIENS,
touchant l'vtilité des Pseaumes.

O Gentils cœurs, & ames amoureuses,
S'il en fut onq, quãd serez langoureuses
D'infirmité, prison, peché, souci,
Perte, ou opprobre, arrestez-vous ici
Espece n'est de tribulation,
Qui n'ait ici sa consolation.
C'est vn iardin plein d'herbes & racines,
Ou de tous maux se trouuent medecines.

O bien-heureux qui voir pourra
Fleurir le temps, que lon orra

Le laboureur à sa charrue,
Le charretier parmi la rue,
Et l'artisan en sa boutique,
Auec vn Pseaume ou Cantique
En son labeur se soulager.
Heureux qui orra le berger
Et la bergere, és bois estans,
Faire que rochers & estangs
Apres eux chantent la hauteur
Du sainct Nom de leur Createur.

CL. MAROT.

Beatus vir qui non abiit.
PSEAVME I. CL. MAR.
¶Ce Pseaume chante que ceux sont bien-heureux qui
reiettans les meurs & le conseil des mauuais, s'adon
nent à cognoistre & mettre à effect la Loy de Dieu:
& mal-heureux ceux qui font au contraire.

Vi au conseil des

ma lins n'a e sté 2 Qui n'est au trac des

pecheurs arre sté, 3 Qui des moqueurs au

banc place n'a pri se 4 Mais nuit & iour

la Loy contéple & pri se 5 De l'E ter

nel, & en est de si reux. 6 Certai ne-

ment ce stuy-la est heu reux.

Et si sera semblable à l'arbrisseau
Planté au long d'vn clair courant ruisseau,
Et qui son fruict en sa saison apporte,
Duquel aussi la fueille ne chet morte:
Si qu'vn tel homme, & tout ce qu'il fera
Tousiours heureux & prospere sera.

Ia les peruers n'auront telles vertus,
Ainçois seront semblables aux festus,
Et à la poudre au gré du vent chassee:
Parquoy sera leur cause renuersee
En iugement, & tous ces reprouuez
Au reng des bons ne seront point trouuez.

Car l'Eternel les iustes cognoit bien:
Et est songneux & d'eux & de leur bien:
Pourtant auront felicité qui dure.
Et pour autant qu'il n'ha ne soin ne cure
Des mal viuans, le chemin qu'ils tiendront,
Eux & leurs faits en ruine viendront.

Quare fremuerunt gentes.
PSEAV. II. CL. MAR.
¶Ici voit-on cõment Dauid & son royaume sont vraye
figure & indubitable prophetie de Iesus Christ & de
son regne.

Our quoy font bruit &

PAGE FROM THE FRENCH PSALTER OF 1556

(See p. 21)

Marot remained in Geneva for a year. But he found life there intolerable. His opinion of the city, expressed in a short poem addressed to the King, is completely contrary to that of Knox, who thought it not far short of a heaven on earth, a 'perfyt schoole of Chryst'. Temperamentally Calvin and Marot were absolute opposites—the one severe, autocratic, intolerant of difference, and in manner of life ascetic; the other a courtier and man of the world, genial, finding friends and associates in quarters which Calvin regarded with frowning disapproval. The only point of contact between them was their common adherence to the Reformed Faith and their interest in enlarging the resources of psalmody. Calvin barely mentions Marot twice in his letters—a significant indication of the degree of good feeling between them; but he valued Marot's serviceableness for his purpose sufficiently to ask the Council to give Marot an official commission to complete the Psalter. When 'that parsimonious body refused to grant the necessary remuneration' Marot threw off the restraints of his uncongenial surroundings and in 1543 withdrew, first to Chambéry and then to Turin, where he died in 1544—allegedly by poison —and was buried in the church of St. John.

The loss of his help brought the growth of the French Psalter to a halt. Five years passed before a successor to him appeared, in the person of Theodore de Bèze— Beza—who arrived in Geneva in October 1548. After a frivolous and dissipated young manhood, he had been brought by a serious illness to a spiritual experience which changed his life to its foundations. With

c

whole-hearted conviction he embraced the Reformed Faith and betook himself to Geneva. Calvin was so much impressed by his scholarship and ability that he offered him the Chair of Greek in the University of Lausanne. Before he left Geneva to take up this office, however, Calvin, calling at his lodging one day in his absence, saw lying on his table the manuscript of a translation of the 16th Psalm into French metre. Taking this away with him, Calvin showed it to his friends, and the consequence was a request to Beza to continue Marot's work and complete the translation and versification of the Psalms. The commission was accepted, and in 1551 thirty-four of Beza's versions were published. Eleven years more were to elapse before the task was finished, but in 1562 the French Psalter was complete.

Marot was indubitably a poet of high distinction. His is the most notable name among the French poets of his age. He 'effected on the versification of his time the first of the changes which were to issue in an actual system which endured for two centuries'. Beza was not a poet, but a theologian. As such, he was of an intellectual and spiritual eminence to make him the inevitable successor to Calvin in the leadership of the French Reformed Church. But it is a measure of the range of his endowments that he was able adequately to continue and complete Marot's work upon the Psalter. Doubtless he was fully aware that in poetic merit he fell far short of Marot's level, but in scholarship there was no shortcoming. For one thing, he knew Hebrew, as Marot did not. And there could be no

more signal evidence of his success in the task entrusted
to him than this, that the Marot–Beza Psalter of 1562
continues to this day, with inconsiderable modifications, to be used by the Protestant Church of France
as its manual of praise.

This long-continued acceptance is the more remarkable because there was a great variety in the metric
and stanzaic forms employed. The aim seems to have
been to impart a distinct individuality to every set of
words and every tune. There are no fewer than 110
metres and 125 tunes. Two-thirds of the stanza-forms
have either six or eight lines; the shortest line consists
of four syllables, the longest of twelve or even thirteen.
The proportion of feminine endings (with the accent
on the second last syllable instead of on the last) is
notably high—about three-eighths of all the lines.
The groupings by rhyme have also a wide variety.
There is nothing in other Psalters to compare with this
deliberate ingenuity in using every kind of structural
device to render impossible the monotony so characteristic of the Psalters used in England, Scotland, and
America.[1]

The musicians achieved a corresponding abundance
in variety. At the time when the Psalter was produced
the ancient modal system, derived in all probability
from a Greek origin, still ruled musical practice, but a
transition from it, in form and spirit, had already
begun. The eight—or, as some hold, fourteen—modes

[1] For a masterly discussion of the metrical forms used and of the
melodies written for them, see *The Music of the French Psalter of 1562: a
Historical Survey and Analysis*, by Dr. Waldo Selden Pratt (New York:
Columbia University Press, 1939).

of tradition were being gradually displaced by the major and minor keys of modern usage. The French Psalter shows this change actually in process. Douen divides its tunes into three classes in respect of modes: (1) *la tonalité antique* (Gregorian), fifty-two tunes; (2) *le mode mineur sans note sensible* (that is, corresponding to the descending melodic minor)—thirty-five tunes; and (3) *le mode majeur* (that is, major)—thirty-eight tunes. Already the majority were more modern than antique, and this predominance was to increase as time went on, until by the end of the sixteenth century the new system prevailed. In the result, with the two systems interpenetrating and blending, and adapting themselves to the wide varieties of metre and stanza in the poetic forms, we may justly say of the music of this Psalter, 'Here is richness': no other comes near it in either poetic or musical accomplishment and interest. All subsequent metrical Psalters are based upon it, and, even though the gulf dividing them is sometimes of the widest, derive from it much of their musical value.

The credit for this musical masterpiece was late in being bestowed in the proper quarter. Many of its tunes used to be confidently ascribed to Guillaume Franc.[1] It is an extenuation of this injustice that Franc preceded the man to whom the honour rightly belongs, as cantor (*chantre*) at Saint-Pierre in Geneva. But his responsibility there was mainly that of teaching the children, giving an hour daily to this exercise. In August 1545 he left Geneva for Lausanne. Already, there, before his arrival, certain Psalms had come into

[1] Or, Le Franc.

use to tunes composed by Gindron, a canon of the cathedral. They were easier tunes, apparently, than those favoured in Geneva. Lausanne preferred to take its own way, and issued a Psalter with tunes from various sources, of which only twenty-seven are assumed to have been written by Franc himself. These found none but local favour: the Psalter in which they appeared never came much into use; and it is clear that Franc had no share in the musical editorship of the historic Psalter of Geneva.

Neither had Claude Goudimel, to whom Scottish music-books of the late eighteenth and early nineteenth centuries ascribed many of the Genevan melodies. Baseless also is the assertion that this distinguished musician opened in Rome the first public school of music apart from the cathedrals and so 'laid the foundation of Italian melodic music'. He did compose five Masses and other works before he cast in his lot with the Reformed religion. But the 1562 French Genevan Psalter captured his interest; thereafter he harmonized many of its tunes in motet form for four or five parts. The complete Psalter, as arranged by him, appeared in 1565: *Les Pseaumes mis en rime francoise par Clement Marot et Theodore de Beze, mis en musique à quatre parties par Claude Goudimel. Par les héritiers de François Jaqui, 1565.* These arrangements were intended, not for public but, as the composer himself said, for private use. For that purpose they were long used by the people, for Rousseau, writing of the peasants of Neuchâtel, two centuries later, said: 'One of their common amusements is to sing the psalms in four parts, with their wives and children, and one is astonished to hear the vigorous and manly harmonies of Goudimel, so long forgotten by our learned musicians, issuing from these country cottages.' Goudimel paid for his adhesion to the Reformed cause by sacrificing his life: he fell a victim of the massacre of the Huguenots at Lyons, in August 1572, five days after the St. Bartholomew massacre in Paris.

The crown of this composer's labours for the Reformed psalmody was to have been an elaborate treatment of the Genevan melodies as the subjects of motets and other pieces arranged for from three to eight voices. Only the last three books of the series planned by him survive. But for the melodies themselves he had no responsibility: he composed for them, after the complete 1562 Psalter was available, choral settings only.

The man who gave this Psalter its distinguished musical character is now known, thanks to the researches of M. Douen, to have been Louis Bourgeois. Appointed to Saint-Pierre in 1545 as cantor in succession to Franc, he had already been charged with the editorship of the music of the Psalter in 1542, and continued to be responsible for successive editions until 1557. Some seventy tunes appear to have been added under his editorship to those already in use in Geneva. How many he actually composed, how many borrowed and adapted, how many he developed from sacred and from secular melodies, are questions to which there is no answer.

Douen, in the first volume of his great work on the

Huguenot Psalter,[1] has a learned chapter on the origins of these tunes, and gives many phrases of popular melodies which make their appearance in them. It does not follow, however, that the tunes have been borrowed from such sources; it has been remarked that the phrases in question 'may merely be a portion of the common property of the time.'[2]

It was a common practice then to make use of 'motto-lines', taken sometimes from secular *chansons* or from well-known ecclesiastical melodies. Thus the same motto-line which introduces Psalm 134 in the French Psalter, in the Anglo-Genevan Psalter introduces Psalm 100 and Psalm 68 also, the rest of the melody developing differently in each case. Major G. A. Crawford[2] is quite justified in saying of the tune known to us as 'Old Hundredth', that 'its component parts are found over and over again in various combinations, and, while one of the most effective, it is also perhaps one of the least original tunes in the Genevan Psalter'.

Bourgeois's fertility in varieties of musical device is astonishing. To take one example: the much-discussed so-called 'gathering-note' in the earliest Scottish psalm-tunes is derived from one type of line-formation of which he made much use. This type begins and ends with long notes, between which several other notes, usually shorter, are strung as on a chain in the middle. There are thirty-five patterns of this class, covering no less than sixty per cent. of the total number of lines. The notes in the middle were not uniformly short as

---

[1] O. Douen, *Clément Marot et le Psautier Huguenot* (Paris, 2 vols., 1878–9).
[2] *The Musical Times*, 1 August 1881.

it is the modern way to make them in tunes of this sort: freedom was used as need required to vary the rhythm. Examples of great interest may be found in the original forms of OLD 100TH and OLD 124TH:

OLD 100TH

OLD 124TH

Thus the term 'gathering-note' is a misnomer, covering a modern misunderstanding of what was really a masterly musical device to impart variety and interest to the rhythm, which is a chief element in the beauty of the tunes to which it is applied.

Bourgeois's task was far from easy. At one point the Council threw him into prison for daring, without their permission, to alter certain of the Strasburg melodies. Calvin at once secured his release, and saw to it that Bourgeois's emendations were accepted. Calvin gave the composer steady and strong support, except in one particular: the reformer was inflexibly opposed to choral singing in public worship, and the Church was as firm as he in rejecting any addition to the simple melody. Bourgeois felt keenly the limitations thus imposed on him, and in 1547, suggestively enough, not at Geneva but at Lyons, he published independently *Pseaulmes cinquante de David, Roy et Prophete, traduictz en vers francois par Clement Marot, et mis en musique par Loys Bovrgeoys, à quatre parties, à voix de contrepoinct egal consonnante au verbe*. In a dedication he says:

'. . . since by the divine grace we have certain psalms of David translated by the late Clement Marot, of eternal memory, in such a happy style that to understand them we need no longer have recourse to foreign tongues, and that they have already begun to be sung in several places, I have thought I could not do anything better or more agreeable to those who take pleasure in praising God with the voice and understanding (as the apostle says) than adapt to the subject and the ordinary tune of the said psalm three parts in harmony, setting note against note. And although the charm and delicacy of music would draw me away from this undertaking, nevertheless I have not given encouragement to this counsel. For it seemed to me that this effeminate music, which is fitted to express either the pleasure or the languor of love, is not suitable to these holy and divine affections.'

Calvin's opposition to the use of choral singing may have been partly grounded upon the expense of printing, and possibly, also, upon doubt whether harmonic practice, then steadily changing, had become sufficiently settled to justify using more than the melody in church; but ultimately, in 1557, Bourgeois became so discouraged that he shook the dust of Geneva off his feet and returned to Paris. There, in 1561, he published settings of eighty-three of the Marot and Beza psalms, for four, five, and six voices; but there is no evidence that these attracted favour, and with their publication he disappears from view.

During the last five years of the development of the French Psalter Bourgeois had no responsibility for the music, and Douen is of opinion that the editor during that time was Pierre Dubuisson, Bourgeois's successor in office as cantor. But it was Bourgeois's work that gave the music of this Psalter its high distinction. Robert Bridges was undoubtedly right in saying that 'Historians who wish to gain a true philosophical account of Calvin's influence at Geneva ought probably to refer a great part of it to the enthusiasm attendant on the singing of Bourgeois's melodies.'

Chapter 3

The Anglo-Genevan Psalter, 1561

IN Geneva, which, under Calvin, had won the reputation of being the most enlightened community in Europe, a company of refugees from England formed a congregation on 1 November 1558. Their ministers were John Knox, made a citizen *ex gratia*, and Goodman, admitted to citizenship 'at his own request'. In the following year, for use in their services, they published a Book of Order, explicitly stated to be the one rejected at Frankfort in favour of the Book of Common Prayer: *The forme of prayers and ministration of the Sacraments, &c. used in the Englishe Congregation at Geneva: and approved by the famous and godly learned man, Iohn Calvyn . . . M.D.LVI.* In course of time it came to be known as 'The Order of Geneva', and also as 'The Book of Common Order', a name subsequently to be transferred to familiar use in Scotland.

The eleventh section of this book bore the title: *One and Fiftie Psalmes of David, in Englishe metre, whereof 37 were made by Thomas Sterneholde, ād the rest by others. cōferred with the hebrewe, and in certeyn places corrected as the text and sens of the Prophete required. Iam. V.* 'Yf any be afflicted, let him pray, and if any be merye, let him singe Psalmes'. These Psalms were at once accepted as the first portion of a Psalter for English use, corresponding to the French one of Marot and Beza, then moving slowly toward completion.

Thomas Sternhold was born at Awre in Gloucester-shire, or, as some say, in Hampshire, and educated at Christ Church, Oxford. He became one of the gentle-men of the Privy Chamber of Henry VIII, and then of Edward VI. He was sincerely religious, and, like Marot, began to produce versified versions of the Psalms with-out any thought of publication. Whether he had seen any of Marot's Psalms, which appear to have been handed about freely in manuscript, is not certain, but it is likely that he had, and it is even asserted that internal evidence supports this probability. But while his versions were written primarily for his own 'godly solace', he hoped that they would serve others also for religious edification, beguiling his fellow-courtiers from the obscene songs they were accustomed to sing, and weaning the people from the ballads, similarly tainted, then current among them. He chose therefore to write his Psalms in ballad-metre, that of 'Chevy Chase', to make it easy for them to be sung to popular melodies such as gave half their charm to the songs whose popularity he wished to counteract. His only chance of getting his verses sung depended upon his giving them something of the same simple, captivat-ing, memorable quality that helped people's memories to take easy and firm hold upon the ballads.

One day in the palace at Whitehall he was singing them privately to his own organ accompaniment when the young lad who within a few years was to succeed to the throne as King Edward VI heard them and was deeply moved; such singing of the sacred words in the common tongue he had never heard before. To whom, then, could Sternhold more fitly dedicate his published Psalms than to this godly prince; and in doing so what better could he say than this ? 'Trusting that as your Grace taketh pleasure to hear them song sometimes of me, so ye will also delyght not only to see and read therein your selfe, but also to commande them to be songe to you of others: that as ye have the psalme it self in your mynde, so ye maye judge myne endeavoure by your care.'

The first instalment published bore the title: *Certayne PSALMES chosē out of the PSALTER OF DAVID and drawē into English metre, by Thomas Sternhold, Grome of ye Kynges Maiesties roobes. Excudebat Londini Edvardus Whitchurche.* This also appears on the title-page: 'Very meete to be used of all sorts of people privately for their solace and comfort, laying apart all ungodly Songes and Ballades, which tend only to the nourishment of vyce and corrupting of Youthe.'

Sternhold's expressed hope of 'travaylying further' and 'performing the residue' of the Psalter was not to be fulfilled: within a few months he was dead. But an admirer was ready to carry the work on. The first edition, undated, contained nineteen Psalms; a second, published posthumously in 1549, contained thirty-seven; a third, in 1557, contained seven others, by J. H. This was John Hopkins (d. 1570), a clergyman and schoolmaster in Suffolk, who is careful to deprecate comparison of his own work with Sternhold's. He publishes his versions, he says,

'not to the intent that they should bee fathered on the dead man, and so through his estimacion to bee the more hyghly esteemed: neyther for that they are in myne opinion, as touching the metre, in any part to be compared with his most exquisite doinges. But especially for that they are fruiteful, although they bee not fine, and comfortable unto a Christyan mind, although not so pleasaunt in the mouthe or eare.'

Hopkins's work is cruder than his predecessor's, though Warton ranks it higher. He is certainly more skilful in rhyming than Sternhold. Usually, he makes the first and third lines of each stanza rhyme, as well as the second and fourth. But the result is often unfortunate.

The 72nd Psalm, verse 1, he renders thus:

> Lord, give thy judgements to the King,
>   therein instruct him well,
> And with his son, that Princely *thing*,
>   Lord, let thy justice dwell.

And the 74th Psalm gives verse 11 thus:

> Why dost thou draw thy hand aback
>   and hid it in thy lap ?
> Oh, pluck it out, and bee not slacke
>   to give thy foes *a rap*.

Much derision has been directed upon Sternhold's work, and it is not difficult to find reasons enough for deriding it. But he seldom descends to doggerel; nor does he often let the exigences of rhyme and metre drive him, as they did Hopkins, into the ludicrous. And there is a straightforward simplicity in his lines which largely accounts for their appeal to the common people. Occasionally he rises to the verge of the poetic, as in these lines from his fine version of the 18th Psalm:

The Lord descended from above,
and bowd the heavens hie;
And underneath his feete hee cast
the darknesse of the skie.
On Cherubs and on Cherubins
full royally he rode,
And on the wings of all the winds
came flying all abroad.

In fairness, it ought to be remembered also that up to that time England had had no great poet but Chaucer, and that Sternhold died fifteen years before Shakespeare was born. As Wood and Fuller put it, 'poetry was in the non-age' then. Moreover, as yet

'the accentuation of English words was in a great measure un-settled; that code of rhymes which now regulates our meanest poetaster had not yet been framed and sanctioned: the grammar of the language was arbitrary and fluctuating; and Shakespeare himself knew not the right superlative degree, and sinned not a little—he and many others—in the use of rhymes now disused and proscribed'.

The first Psalter for the Anglo-Genevan Church appeared in 1556, containing fifty-one Psalms, with tunes. The Psalms were the forty-four of Sternhold and Hopkins, with seven new ones, known to have been by Whittingham. Another edition appeared in 1558, containing sixty-two Psalms, of which nine were by Whittingham and two by his friend Pullain. Three more were added in the 1560 edition. These were all retained in the next edition of 1561 and in the completed Scottish Psalter of 1564. This last edition contained other noteworthy additions: twenty-five fresh Psalms signed W. Ke (William Kethe), including

'All people that on earth do dwell' to its familiar tune, which had already appeared, set to Psalm 134 in the 1551 French Psalter; including also a version of 'The Song of Simeon', two versions of the Lord's Prayer, known to have been by Whittingham, and a third, of the same Prayer, anonymous, but known to have been by Cox, Whittingham's chief adversary at Frankfort.

Of the three new contributors of psalm-versions John Pullain was of least consequence. His versions of Psalms 148 and 149, however, are vigorously done. The former is specially notable for its fine metre—that of Watts's 'Lord of all worlds above'. Both passed into the Scottish Psalter of 1564.

William Whittingham, born at Chester in 1524, and educated at Oxford, was won to the Reformed faith during subsequent continental travels, and became one of its most resolute supporters. He stood by Knox in the Frankfort disputations, and in 1555 followed him to Geneva. He was easily the most influential layman among the continental exiles, and the natural leader of the Geneva group, which probably never numbered more than 200 persons though the effects of its work were so far-reaching. He married Calvin's sister Catherine, and ultimately, under the urgent pressure of Calvin, accepted ordination. Literary work constantly occupied him: he was chiefly responsible for the translation known as the Geneva Bible, which had a large circulation in England and Scotland.

His contributions to the Psalter were of very varying quality. Our debt to him is great for the stirring second version of Psalm 124, 'Now Israel may say, and that truly'. Its rugged strength is perfectly matched by the noble Genevan melody, and in the revised form of 1650 it is sung with fervour in Scotland to this day. Honour is due to him also for the version of Psalm 23 which to the 'beautiful and serene' eight-line tune of Psalm 3 was the first version popularly sung in Scotland:

> The Lord is only my support,
>   and hee that doth me feede:
> How can I then lacke anie thing
>   whereof I stand in need?
> Hee doth me fold in coates most safe,
>   the tender grasse fast by:
> And after driv'th me to the streames
>   which run most pleasantly.
>
> And when I feele my self neare lost,
>   then doth hee mee home take:
> Conducting mee in his right pathes,
>   even for his own Names sake.
> And though I were even at deaths doore,
>   yet would I feare none ill:
> For by thy rod, and sheepheards crooke
>   I am comfórted still.
>
> Thou hast my table richly deckt
>   in despite of my fo:
> Thou hast mine head with balme refresht,
>   my cup doth over-flow.
> And finally, while breath doth last,
>   thy grace shall mee defend:
> And in the house of God will I
>   my life for ever spend.

Where Whittingham failed was in his attempts to make

D

singable versions to French metres. Miss Anne G. Gilchrist justly says:

'Give Whittingham an English tune and an English metre to fit it, and instead of breaking his teeth on the French metrical forms, how well he can use long, short, or common measure, as in his spirited Psalm 114, either as sung to its proper tune in the Scottish Psalter or to the tune we now know as the Old 44th.'[1]

The same difficulty beset William Kethe, author of the now universally known second version of the 100th Psalm, 'All people that on earth do dwell'. Both Warton in his *History of English Poetry* and Strype in his *Annals of the Reformation* say that he was a Scotsman, but no confirmatory particulars of his birth, family, or early history are known. He was much trusted as a negotiator by the scattered groups of exiles on the Continent, and was also in high repute as a scholar. When these refugees, 'dispersed in sundry places of Germany and Helvetia', prepared to return home after Queen Mary's death, 'certaine . . . remained behinde the reste, to witt, to finishe the Bible and the psalmes, both in meeter and prose, which were already begoon, at the charges of such as were of most habilitie in that congregation' (Geneva). Kethe was one of those who remained. His special task was to carry onward the metrical version of the Psalter, for all the twenty-five additions published in 1561 were from his pen.[2]

Unfortunately no fewer than eighteen of these twenty-five versions were written for French tunes. Transla-

[1] Anne G. Gilchrist: 'Psalm-Versions and French Tunes in the Scottish Psalter of 1564', in *Records of the Scottish Church History Society*, v. 308.

[2] These were: 27, 36, 47, 54, 58, 62, 70, 85, 88, 90, 91, 94, 100, 101, 104, 107, 111, 112, 113, 122, 125, 126, 134, 138, and 142.

tion presents formidable difficulties when poetry has
to be turned from French into English that can be sung:
differences of accentuation in the two languages, and
particularly the stumbling-block of French feminine
endings and sounded final e's, require exceptional
skill to negotiate. The French Psalter increased the
translators' embarrassments by setting them the problem of accommodating a large variety of unfamiliar
metres to English verse-forms. The failures of Whittingham in this field were equalled by those of Kethe.
This explains partly why only one version of each—
albeit both are of a high order—was accepted by the
editors of the 1650 Psalter: the peculiar metres imposed
by the French originals put the others out of court:
none of the ordinary tunes would match them, and the
two accepted had to go in as second versions.

Where the original tunes of the Anglo-Genevan
Psalter came from, no one can tell. Musicians at that
time were not eager to claim the credit of their compositions; and if it be true, as Bishop Frere surmised,
that the first tunes which set the standard for the
rest went, already made, from England to Geneva
along with the Sternhold and Hopkins Psalms, it is
easy to understand why, in the conditions of the time,
their composers had no desire to draw attention to their
Protestant sympathies. Frere's supposition would
partly explain why the Anglo-Genevan tunes, except
at the last, were not more markedly affected by those
of the French Psalter, and set a standard of their own.
But the Sternhold and Hopkins favour for common
metre of course imposed an unavoidable uniformity

on these earlier tunes. The preponderance of D.C.M. tunes was unfortunate, and, though it had before long to be departed from, it left an abiding mark in the eight-line verse-form in which the metrical Psalms are almost invariably printed still. It is remarkable that so few tunes of this time and class survive in present-day use, though the solidity and strength of them are beyond dispute.[1]

The year 1560 ended the Anglo-Genevan Church. In that year not a single English family was left in Geneva: all returned home when Queen Mary died. Whittingham, in spite of his Presbyterian ordination and firm adherence to the Puritan party, accepted the Book of Common Prayer, became Dean of Durham, and after a troublous tenure of that office, died in 1579. Kethe became rector of Childe Okeford, Devon, in 1561, and there remained till his death in 1593. Pullain became Archdeacon of Colchester, and died in 1565.

[1] See Indexes of Composers, &c., in *The Scottish Psalter 1929,* and *The Revised Church Hymnary 1927* for examples of Anglo-Genevan tunes.

Chapter 4

The English Psalter, 1562

THE influence of this Psalter upon the Scottish one of 1564 was limited. Both started from the same point—the Anglo-Genevan Psalter, but in 1558 differences of tendency began to appear, which ended in wide divergences in both words and music.

When, in 1558, Queen Mary died, and many of those in voluntary exile during her reign returned to England, the Anglo-Genevan Psalter was not yet completed. Some collaborators, led by Kethe, remained in Geneva to carry the work forward. But simultaneously a group appears to have been formed among those who returned to England, to address themselves to the same task. Each group appears to have proceeded in ignorance of what the other was doing. Probably also, differences of view, latent since the troubles at Frankfort, came into operation, and took effect in differentiating in marked ways the results of the work upon which the two groups were engaged. From what was done in Geneva the Scottish Psalter of 1564 took shape; the Scottish General Assembly accepted the Genevan results *en bloc*. From the independent work in England there developed another Psalter, modifying the Genevan results and aiming definitely at suitability for use with the Book of Common Prayer.

The first English Psalter was printed by John Daye in 1559, but as no licence for it had been obtained he was fined, and it is doubtful whether it was ever published; no copy is known to exist. Another was issued in 1560, containing sixty-five Psalms and a significant appendix, embodying metrical versions of the *Magnificat*, the *Benedictus*, the *Nunc Dimittis*, 'the XII Articles of the Christen fayth', the Lord's Prayer in Cox's version, and Whittingham's version of the Ten Commandments, with the 'Addition' of the response 'Lord, have mercy upon us', &c. In 1561 John Daye's second Psalter appeared, containing eighty-seven Psalms, and new versions of the Canticles, &c., showing still more clearly the deliberate intention to draw the Psalter into conformity with the use of the Prayer Book. In 1562 the process was completed by the issue, by Daye, of the definitive edition which was to remain in use in England until well into the nineteenth century: *The Whole Booke of Psalmes, collected into Englysh metre by T. Starnhold, I. Hopkins, and others : conferred with the Ebrue, with apt Notes to synge thē withal, Faithfully perused and alowed according to thordre appointed in the Quenes maiesties Iniunctions, etc.*

Here we see clearly the respects in which the English development of the Psalter moved away from the course followed in Geneva.

The original forty-four Psalms of Sternhold and Hopkins which had formed the basis of the Anglo-Genevan Psalter are restored to their first form, as in 1549, and Whittingham's emendations are discarded.

Of the forty-three versions added to the Anglo-Genevan version in 1556–61, twenty are retained and twenty-three rejected, and eighty-six new versions appear, including a duplicate version of Psalm 51. Four of the new ones bear Sternhold's name: presumably they were discovered after his death. Hopkins contributes fifty-three of the additions.

The imitations by Whittingham and Kethe of French metres to suit French tunes are sparingly admitted to the English version. Even Kethe's great version of Psalm 100, strangely ascribed to Sternhold in the 1561 Anglo-Genevan Psalter, is omitted from Daye's *Whole Booke of Psalmes* in 1562. It is admitted to an appendix in 1564, and Sternhold's name as author disappears, but Kethe's is not substituted; nor in subsequent editions does Daye give any indication of authorship until 1587, when the misleading initials 'I. H.' are appended.

The English Psalters, by constantly increasing the number of 'Spiritual Songs' prefixed or appended to them, show a steady tendency towards adding to the Psalter 'the nucleus of a hymn-book' for use with the Prayer Book.

In the music the divergence of the two movements is still more marked. The old modal tunes were gradually dropped from the English book, and also most of those that came from the French Psalter. The reaction against Geneva, evident in other ways, sent the editors back to a more distinctive English tradition. The change from the old tonalities might have been a gain if the new tunes had been of a finer quality, but they were not. The reversion was to the heavy style imposed on the one hand by the Reformers' demand for distinct articulation of the words, with one note to a syllable, and on the other by Cranmer's requirement that the harmonizing should be note against note,— that is, in plain chords. The dismissal of the French style, which, even when altered to suit English metres, did not wholly lose its splendour, left the plain D.C.M. style in overwhelming predominance. 'The English tradition hardly ever got away from the jog-trot of D.C.M.; after the modal tunes of that metre had been eliminated, those that remained were for the most part uniformly dull, and those that took the vacant places were certainly not less so.' In the result 'the D.C.M. tunes are repeated *ad nauseam*, for there are more than four times as many of them as of those in peculiar metres'.[1] The dullness became more pronounced as time went on; tunes of this time and type, though still printed, have largely passed out of use.

Though the editors of the Scottish Psalter of 1564 must have realized the divergences of the English book from their own aims, there is no sign of prejudice or resentment being awakened in them. No doubt a shortage of native-born versifiers helped to tone down any adverse feelings; they did not hesitate to borrow from the English book to eke out what their own men could not supply to complete their own version. Two English contributors were drawn upon.

The first, Thomas Norton, called by Wood 'a forward and busy Calvinist', was really much more than that. He has a place in English literature as joint-author with the Earl of Sackville of *Gorboduc*, the first blank-

[1] W. H. Frere, in the Introduction to the Historical Edition of *Hymns Ancient and Modern*, 1909.

verse tragedy in the language. Though lifeless and 'inflexibly stiff . . . it set for ever the pattern for serious drama [in this country] and developed into the marvellous instrument of Shakespeare himself'.[1] In theological literature also Norton had an influential place, as the first translator into English of Calvin's *Institutes of Religion.* The publication of seven complete editions and one abridgement between 1561 and 1599 shows that his translation was much used by readers unable to read the original Latin. Norton contributed twenty-six of the new versions to the English Psalter of 1562, and of these eight were taken over into the Scottish Psalter.

The other English contributor to be noted for our purpose is indicated by the letter M appended to four of the Psalms. For a time it was assumed that this was John Mardley, 'who turned twenty-four psalms into English odes, and made many religious songs'. But in the 1565 Psalter one of the hymns having this initial bears the name Marckant in full, and identifies the writer as John Marckant, incumbent of Clacton Magna (1559), and of Shopland (1563–8). He is known as the writer of a few hymns and other poems, one of which, known as 'The Lamentation' and beginning 'O Lord, turn not away Thy face', appears in modern hymnals, including the *Revised Church Hymnary* (401). Of Marckant's versions contributed to the 1562 English Psalter (118, 131, 132, 135), two (131 and 135) were taken over into the 1564 Scottish Psalter.

[1] George Sampson: *The Concise Cambridge History of English Literature,* p. 153.

To some extent the borrowing was mutual. Assuming Kethe to have been a Scotsman, there were at least nine Scottish contributions to the English Psalter, not including Psalm 100. Kethe's '104th psalm is one of the best in the Psalter, and its metre the only surviving result that has achieved success of the attempts to naturalize the French'.

John Craig was given a late entry: his 136th Psalm was not adopted, from the Scottish Psalter, till 1581, and then, mistakenly, with the initials 'T. C.' which concealed his identity until Dr. Livingston discovered the error. In all, the Scottish Psalter selected forty-two versions from the eighty-six new translations in the English Psalter of 1562. These were all subjected to very careful revision.

There was free borrowing on both sides in the music. The following tunes, common to both, are almost certainly Scottish: OLD COMMON, DUKE'S, DUNFERMLINE, MARTYRS, KING'S, FRENCH (DUNDEE), STILT (YORK), ABBEY, GLASGOW[1]; and England has a prior claim to: LONDON (CAMBRIDGE), ENGLISH, MONROS (ROCHESTER), CHESHIRE, DURHAM, WINCHESTER, DUNDEE (WINDSOR or EATON).

[1] Not the tune now known by that name.

II

The First

Scottish

Psalter

1564

Chapter 5

The Composition of the Psalter

OWING to the disappearance of the early records of the Church of Scotland it is impossible to state precisely the facts of the launching of this Psalter. Sternhold and Hopkins's first collection of twenty-four Psalms without music had found its way northward about 1550. The 1558 Psalter, with music, had followed. But a definite Scottish beginning was still to come. Calderwood the historian is our authority for saying that 'In the General Assemblie conveened in Edinburgh in December 1562, for printing of the Psalms, the Kirk lent Robert Lekprevik, printer, tua hundreth punds to help to buy irons, ink and paper, and to fie craftsmen for printing'. This implies that a selection of Psalms was in readiness for immediate use, but that facilities for printing music did not yet exist in Scotland.

Knox was by this time settled in Scotland; he returned in 1559. The first General Assembly was held in 1560; he had part in whatever was decided there. Recognition was given to the Genevan *Forme of Praiers*, &c., of 1556 as 'oure book of Common Ordour' and 'the Ordour of Geneva whilk now is used in some of oure Kirks'. Though these titles connote only the prose documents so named, the inference is natural that the Psalms of that date are also covered by them, and that by that time these were already in partial use in Scotland. The Psalms Lekprevik was commissioned to print were therefore, almost certainly, the fifty-one published at Geneva in 1556. The General Assembly arranged that they should be revised and that the whole Psalter should be completed.

Knox's pre-eminent share in these proceedings warrants the belief that he was a member of the Committee on the Psalms, although his qualifications for speaking with an authoritative voice on either the verse or the music are in considerable doubt. It does not derogate from the honour due to him as the strong leader the nation needed in a time of acute peril for its fortunes, to recognize that there is no evidence in him of sensitivity to music or poetry. 'With all his continental experience, he had been untouched by the Renaissance. . . . He had learned nothing of Roman moderation or Roman orderliness. He had no Greek sense of beauty. There was not a spark of poetry in his outlook. He had no tears for human affairs.'[1]

Who his collaborators were upon the Psalter is not told us, but the identity of two of them stands beyond question, for they were the only Scottish contributors of new versions—Robert Pont and John Craig.

Pont must have been a man of eminent gifts. He was a member of the first General Assembly and stepped at once into the front rank of the Church's notabilities. He became minister of Dunblane, then Commissioner of Moray. In 1570 he was presented to St. Cuthbert's,

[1] Wallace Notestein, *The Scot in History* (Jonathan Cape, London, 1946), p. 120.

Edinburgh, and in 1571, by special permission of the Church, was raised to the bench as a Senator of the College of Justice. For twelve years he fulfilled the duties of these two offices. Offered the bishopric of Caithness in 1587, he declined. He died in 1608.

Six psalm-versions by him appear in the 1564 Psalter.[1] These were mostly in peculiar metres. 'Pont's verses are about as awkward as possible', says Miss A. G. Gilchrist with justice. If he got the requisite number of syllables into the lines of his translations from the French, he does not seem to have cared whether they suited the music or not; his skill as a translator is as small as Kethe's or Whittingham's. Some of his versions defy the efforts of even skilled choirs to fit them to their proper melodies. The metres he had to deal with made his versions unsuitable for transference to the 1650 Psalter.

The story of the other Scottish contributor, John Craig, is of romantic interest. Of the family of Craig of Craigston, Aberdeenshire, he was born in 1512. The year after his birth his father fell at Flodden. After studying at St. Andrews he became a Dominican monk. Under suspicion of heresy he was for a short time imprisoned and had to flee. Proceeding to Rome, he obtained the interest of Cardinal Pole, and was appointed master of the novices in the monastery of his order at Bologna. In the library there he found a copy of Calvin's *Institutes,* and underwent so complete a change of mind that he adopted the Reformed faith. He left the monastery, but was seized by the Inquisi-

[1] Psalms 57, 59, 76, 80, 81, 83.

tion and committed to prison in Rome. There for nine months he lay, as John Row relates, 'in a sort of pit, into the whilk the river Tibris did every tide flow, so that the prisoners stood in water sometimes almost to their middles'. The Inquisition condemned him to be burned on 19 August 1559, but the death of Pope Paul IV three days earlier caused a tumult, in the course of which the prison was thrown open and Craig escaped. Through many adventures he made his way back to Scotland, and reached Edinburgh in 1560.

Twenty-four years of residence abroad and constant use of Latin made it difficult for him to preach in his own Scots tongue; so at first he conducted services in Latin, attended by the learned men of the city, in the Magdalen Chapel in the Cowgate. But in 1561 he became minister of Holyrood (Canongate), and in 1562 colleague to Knox in St. Giles's. In 1570 he was Moderator of the General Assembly. After a brief ministry in Montrose he was sent to Aberdeen 'to illuminate those dark places in Mar, Buchan, and Aberdeen, and to teach the youth of the college there'. Returning to Edinburgh in 1580 he became one of the ministers of the King's House, and in 1581, for the second time, Moderator of Assembly. He continued to hold office in Holyrood until, full of years and honours, he died at the age of eighty-eight, in December 1600.

Craig's fifteen contributions to the Psalter[1] vary much in quality, but the second version of Psalm 145, which still remains second only to Kethe's 100th in

[1] Psalms 24, 56, 75, 102, 105, 108, 110, 117, 118, 132, 136, 140, 141, 143, 145.

PSALME XXXIIII. THO. STER.

¶ After Dauid had escaped Achis, according as is written in the
1. Sa. 21. whome in this tytle he calleth Abimelech (which was
a generall Name to all the Kings of the Philistims) he praiseth
God for his deliuerance, prouoking all others by his example to
trust in God, to feare and serue him, who defendeth the godly
with his Angels, and vtterly destroyeth the wicked in their sin-
nes.

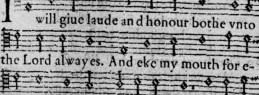

I will giue laude and honour bothe vnto

the Lord alwayes. And eke my mouth for e-

uer more shal speak vnto his praise, I do de-

lite to laude the Lord in soule and eke in

voyce, That humble men and mortified may

beare and so reioyce.

3 Therefore se that ye magnifie,
    with me the liuing Lord,
    And let vs now exalt his Name
     together with one accorde.
4 For I my self besoght the Lord:

                  he an-

PAGE FROM THE SCOTTISH PSALTER, 1564

O *Lrd, the plentifull heip of all happines, sen it hes*
plesit the of thy free mercie and gudeneſſe, to chuſe
vs for thy avvin heritage, and to regener vs ſpiritually
Entertaine vs vnder thy vvings vnto the end: & grant
that vve may dailie grovve in the knavvledge of thy
gudeneſſe, trouth, and mercie, quhilkis thou hes mani-
feſted vnto vs, through our Redeemer, and Sauiour Ie-
ſus Chriſt. Sʒ be it.

PSALME CI. W. Ke.

¶ Dauid deſcribeth what gouernement hee will obſerue in his
houſe & kingdome, be ruting out the wickit, & cheriſhing the godly.

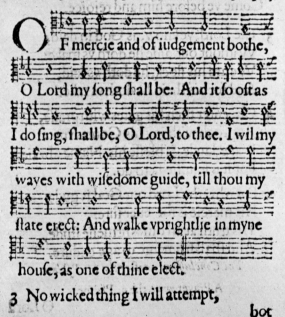

Of mercie and of iudgement bothe,
O Lord my ſong ſhall be: And it ſo oſt as
I do ſing, ſhall be, O Lord, to thee. I wil my
wayes with wiſedome guide, till thou my
ſtate erect: And walke vprightlie in myne
houſe, as one of thine elect.

3 No wicked thing I will attempt,

bot

---

use and honour, is a conclusive evidence of his powers. So also, although much altered in 1650, are his notable second versions of Psalms 136 and 143.

Summing up the results of the intricate pedigree of the Psalter, it is found that 39 versions were Sternhold's, 37 Hopkins's, 16 Whittingham's, 25 Kethe's, 2 Pullain's, 8 Norton's, 2 Marckant's, 15 Craig's, and 6 Pont's. The majority therefore were English, though with some revision, and, assuming that Kethe was really a Scotsman, only 46 were of Scottish authorship.

The completed Psalter appeared under this title: *The Forme Of Prayers And Ministration Of The Sacraments etc. used in the English Church at Geneva, approved and received by the Churche of Scotland, whereunto besydes that was in the former bokes, are also added sondrie other prayers, with the whole Psalmes of David in English meter. . . . Printed At Edinburgh By Robert Lekprevik M.D.LXIIII.*

The versification of this Psalter as a whole has the characteristics of its time. There was little that was poetic in it; the aim was rather to give a close rendering of the original text than to satisfy the modern conceptions of good poetry. Thomas Fuller was right in saying that the versifiers 'had drunk more of Jordan than of Helicon; sometimes they made the Maker of the tongue speak little better than barbarism, and have in many verses such poor rhime that two hammers on a smith's anvil would have made better music'. And as another critic said, 'The wording is flat and homely, and wholly fails to render the majesty of the Hebrew Psalms.'

The metres used in this Psalter are more varied than

E

those used in the English one: there are twenty-seven of them, some following French originals. This gave the musicians greater scope. Whereas the English Psalter, reducing the French element, had sixty-two tunes for Psalms and appended hymns, the Scottish, which had no appendix of 'Spiritual Songs', had one hundred and five tunes for Psalms alone.

The Reformers wisely aimed at encouraging the people to sing. They recognized that whereas there are some things 'so necessarie that without the same thair is no face of ane visible Kirk', there are others less strictly essential, and among these was the singing of psalms, for 'in some churches, the psalmes may be conveniently sung, in utheris, perchance they can not'. But they started well by printing the tunes with the psalms, and three editions only before 1625 were issued without music; from that date only six out of a total of twenty-nine editions issued up till 1644 contained the tunes.

The music was carefully supervised. Naturally a good deal of use was made of the old modes. Forty-two of the tunes were taken from Geneva; of these, thirty-one were French—among them, happily, some of Bourgeois's finest productions. Only a few were German. Many did not appear in the English Psalter, but which were by Scottish composers it is impossible to say. The melody was given in the C clef only, unison-singing being at first intended alike for congregational and family use. The pitch was not fixed, but was left free for the leader's choice, and the indications are that the speed was not intended to be slow. Many tunes are not well suited to their Psalms, but the whole work was pervaded by a deep religious sense. The secular style, which by and by was to dominate Scottish psalmody, does not appear, nor is the folk-song element allowed to intrude.

Everything possible was done to ensure the general use of the book. A statute required 'that every Minister, Exhorter and Reader, sall have one of the Psalme bookes latelie printed in Edinburgh', and in 1579 an Act of Parliament ordained 'that all Gentlemen with 300 merks of yearlie rent, and all substantious yeomen, etc., worth 500 pounds in lands or goods, be holden to have ane bible and psalme booke' under specified penalties. In Edinburgh security was taken that this law was complied with, for those liable under it were ordered, 'for eschewing of all fraude', to 'bring their bibylls and psalm buiks, to have their names writtin and subscryvit be the clerk'. Large numbers were sold. Including Lekprevik's first edition, sixty-four editions were published between 1562 and 1644, when it had become known that the book was before long to be superseded. If the preceding six editions issued from Geneva be added, the total number of editions published was seventy.

Many of these editions were printed outside of Scotland—at Middelburg, Dort, London, Geneva—doubtless for the same reasons as those stated at the trial of Archbishop Laud, in defence of his interference with the importation of books from the Continent into England: 'The books that came thence were better print, better bound, better paper, and for all the charges of bringing sold better cheap.' Between 1587 and 1601 the majority of editions were printed abroad.

The printers seem to have been allowed great latitude. When the book was published power was given to the Moderator, the Ministers of Edinburgh, and the Clerk, or any three of them, to order the printing and see that the transcription for the press and the printing were well corrected. But as time went on, supervision of the work seems to have been of the most lax description. Various evidences show this. For example, editions printed at Middelburg and Dort, and one in Edinburgh, between 1599 and 1611, omitted many of the proper tunes—in 1602 as many as sixty-one. Yet not till 1611 were the missing tunes restored. Some printers held themselves at liberty to introduce elements which had no Assembly authorization behind them. Thus in Andro Hart's edition of 1615 a metrical version of the Song of Moses appeared, prefaced by this note from the printer:

'Beeing in conference with a Godlie Brother (Christian Reader) I shewed unto him that I was minded to print over againe this Booke of the Psalmes, who saide unto me that he marveled that the Song of Moses was never yet insert therein. . . . I requested him therefore that I might have it put into Meeter, who accorded and sent mee the same to bee insert in this new Edition.'[1]

The period was one of much tension between Presbyterians and Episcopalians, and the appearance in some editions of features akin to those favoured by the latter party does not imply any official sanction for

[1] This version bears the initials I. M., which are known to be James Melville's.

them; it may indicate nothing more than the printer's personal sympathies or the degree of some influential pressure behind him.

Bassandine's edition of 1575 departs from the common usage by giving the book for the first time the title *The CL Psalmes of David*—a feature which was to be permanent and to begin the practice of calling the whole Service Book briefly *The Psalm Book*. In this edition there also appear metrical versions of the Lord's Prayer (Coxe's), Whittingham's Ten Commandments with a responsory prayer, the first Lamentation, and the *Veni Creator* from the English Prayer Book.

Henry Charteris's Edinburgh edition of 1596 is remarkable for several innovations for which he claims personal responsibility. Instead of the usual three divisions of the Contents of the Service Book he makes five, giving 'the discreit Reider' an explanation 'to shaw the occasioun thairof, quhilk is altogidder for the eis and plesour of the byer'. Accordingly, he prints separately 'the haill Psalmes with their praiers following . . . chiefly for the eis of men in travel, and being from thair hame, quha glaidlie wald carie ane thin buik'. The prayers given with the psalms, one for each, are in the finest Scottish diction of the period, and were long supposed to be of genuine Scottish origin, in spite of their being in collect-form—a form not then or ever characteristic of the Scottish Church. They are now known to be translations from the French of Augustin Marlorat, a colleague of Calvin and Beza in the Genevan Reformation. They were printed first in the French Psalter in 1561, and in successive editions until 1674 at least. The author of the Scots version[1] is not known; it appears nowhere but in Charteris's edition.

Charteris printed also in the same edition thirty-two 'Conclusions' or Doxologies (*Gloria Patri*), to suit all the metres of the Psalms. The first of the species appeared in 1575,[2] at the very end of the volume, as to be sung to Psalm 148. In the 1635 Psalter only one is given, for all psalms in common metre. According to Baillie[3] there was a time when they had considerable use and were the subject of much controversy. 'Whether their adoption was in compliance with covert pressure for approximation to Episcopal practices,' says Dr. Livingston, 'or from a spontaneous movement of the Church, are doubtful questions.' Probably, like the French collects, they were inserted on the printer's own responsibility. In 1650 they disappeared completely. Baillie, in a letter dated 25 April 1645,[4] gives the reason, saying that 'in the new translation of the Psalmes, resolving to keep punctuallie to the originall text, without any addition, we and they [the English

[1] See *The Scottish Collects of 1595*, modernized, with an Introduction by the present writer (Church of Scotland Publications Office). In their Scottish form the prayers are printed in full in Livingston's edition of the 1635 Psalter.

[2] The origin of the practice is apparent from the fact that after the Restoration a minister, preaching before Parliament on 27 January 1661, 'restored *Glory to the Father*, to be sung at the end of the Psalmes', and this, it is said in the *Mercurius Caledonius*, 'has been a great stranger to our Kirk these many years'.

[3] See paper from Baillie's unpublished writings in Neil Livingston, *The Scottish Metrical Psalter of A.D. 1635, reprinted in full from the original work, . . . and the whole illustrated by Dissertations, Titles and Facsimiles.* Glasgow, 1864. See Chapter 7.

[4] Livingston, op. cit., p. 36.

Divines] were content to omitt that whereupon we saw both the Popish and Prelaticall partie did so much dote, as to put it to the end of the most of their lessons and all their psalmes'. Unless this last reference is to the prose psalms, Baillie is here mistaken, for 'metrical doxologies do not occur in the English Psalters generally as appendages to the psalms'.[1] Endeavours to resuscitate their use in Scotland have thus far failed, and after 300 years of disuse of them are not likely to succeed. They are not part of the present Scottish tradition, any more than they were of the original Reformation practice, and no one who ever sings them, say to Psalms 23 and 100, will have any doubt in his mind about their being an intrusion, and sometimes an extremely irritating superfluity.

In 1625 the Common Tunes were first published with harmony. Fifteen were given in four parts, with BON ACCORD 'in Reports', in Edward Raban's Aberdeen Psalter of that year. This was the first appearance of harmonized tunes in a Scottish psalm-book.

After 1622, most Psalters published were without music altogether. Among the six with music, it is true, was the outstanding harmonized Psalter of 1635,[2] but its appearance must have been but a dying blaze of splendour, for fifteen years later the 1564 Psalter was dead.

[1] Livingston, op. cit., p. 36.
[2] See Chapter 7.

Chapter 6

The St. Andrews Psalter, 1562–6

IN his *History of Scotland* Andrew Lang raises the question, How did the Catholics take their new fortunes when the Reformation overthrew the whole Scottish structure of their Church?

'Unhappily,' he answers, 'we know very little on the subject. The country must have seemed strangely desolate to souls of the old faith. The familiar shrines were vacant of their saints. "The blessed mutter of the Mass" was silent: the candles were extinguished, the vestments were cut up for doublets, the last incense smoke had rolled away. In lonely cleughs of Ettrickdale the chapels were desecrated; the crosses by the wayside had perished; the Angelus no longer called to prayer; the tombs were stripped and spoiled. If all these things had exercised their ministry in stimulating and consoling and regulating the religious emotions: if the extreme rites of the Church had fortified men in the hour of death—the souls that desired them starved. How much misery this caused we know not, and cannot know.'

Lang, himself no musician, did not gather within the scope of the sympathy thus expressed the people whose calling had been the maintenance of the music of the Church. But *their* plight too must have been grievous. The organs were disused, if not destroyed; the song-schools, where they survived, maintained a precarious and decaying existence, but the whole of the music for the practice and performance of which they had their being was swept away into dishonour and disuse. The stores of their written music ceased to serve any purpose: the service-books—Missal, Antiphonary, Graduals, &c.—became lumber, fit for nothing but destruction. Nothing was left for the song-schools to work upon but the meagre psalm-tunes that came in driblets from Geneva.

Among those who realized that disaster was impending, not for Church music only, but for music generally in Scotland, was Lord James Stewart, afterwards to be famous as the Earl of Moray and Regent of Scotland, 'the good Regent', beloved of the Scottish people. He was a natural son of James V and therefore a half-brother of Queen Mary. Educated at St. Andrews University, though yet a minor at the time of the Reformation, he was Prior of St. Andrews. He embraced the new faith when the choice between the old and the new had to be made. Foreseeing the calamity about to befall music, and determined, as far as possible, to reduce its consequences, he commissioned David Peebles, one of his canons, described as 'ane of the principall musitians in all this land in his tyme' and as 'ane honourable and singulare cunning man', to compose contrapuntal settings for the new psalm-tunes—to 'set three pairtes to the tenor', which was the tune or people's part. Peebles, however, was not given unfettered freedom as to the mode in which this commission was to be carried out. His instruction was to make the music 'plain and dulce', and to avoid 'the curiosity of music', which is to say, ornamentation of every kind with which as a musician he might be tempted to adorn and enrich his work.

It may be imagined that an accomplished master of music, as he was, would be little in love with such a task. He could have little enthusiasm for the Reformation, and small esteem therefore for those 'beggarly elements' its tunes, which represented an immeasurable descent from the splendours of the cathedral music upon which he had long been engaged.[1] He appears, consequently, to have gone laggardly about the business: he was 'not earnest', Wood mildly said. The work dragged and drifted, and probably would never have been done at all if, just at that juncture, Thomas Wode or Wood had not come from Dunbar to Fife as 'vicar of Sanctandrous'.

Wood was not himself a composer, but he had a passionate love for music, and it dismayed him to think of the prospects of 'the art and syence' he loved, under the Reformed regime. He believed, and as the event showed was justified in believing, that music was likely to perish from the land. What Peebles had engaged to do, however, kindled a ray of hope. If only so capable a composer would go ahead and finish his task, something might be saved out of the wreck. So Wood pestered the dilatory canon. He says, 'I was ever requesting and solisting', till the Psalms were all set. Other musicians of eminence[2] whom he names he got to do the same for the Canticles and supplementary 'Spiritual Songs'; but with the exception, possibly,[3] of

[1] About 1530 he set the canticle *Si quis diligit me* in four parts. According to Priory documents quoted by Dr. D. Hay Fleming, he was in residence in St. Andrews in January 1565-6, and in 1571 he and his wife had a house and land there. [2] See p. 63.

[3] Wood's two marginal notes are enigmatic: they make it clear that

two by John Buchan, the 'most honest, quiet and sober' master of the Glasgow Song School, the arrangements for the Psalms were all Peebles's work.

Wood's own part in the Psalter was simply that of a sedulous copyist. As Peebles's arrangements came into his hands, he wrote them out in clear and beautiful script, and preserved the sheets for subsequent binding. He was not satisfied with merely transcribing the music. His manuscript is lavishly adorned with illuminated initial letters at the beginning of each Psalm, and vignettes there and at the end, and also with floreation in the margins. Each part-book had a coloured frontispiece also. All this decorative work was done after the manner of the old illuminated missals, though the fact that paper and not vellum was used, and the colouring materials were of a much less rich and brilliant sort, resulted in less satisfying effects. 'The workmanship of the original is evidently that of a clever and practised penman, but one whose eye has been dimmed and his hand shaken by age.'

Wood followed the custom of his time in engrossing each of the four, and in some cases five, parts in a separate volume. Full scores for choir use were as yet hardly known: each singer had his own part and no other before him. Often such part-books were written on scraps of parchment or of paper, liable to be mislaid or scattered. In the present case each part was carefully entrusted to a part-book, and widely dispersed these part-books came to be. Some found their way, curi-

Buchan borrowed the manuscript and altered it in two instances, but to what extent is not clear.

ously, to Ireland. One, the fifth part (supplementary)[1] is in Trinity College, Dublin. David Laing, the eminent antiquary, acquired two from the library of a clergyman in Kilkenny, and a third, which he obtained from an Edinburgh friend, also came from Ireland. Wood, in a note, says that after he had finished the first set of five books, he prepared a duplicate set, for the inferior artistic quality of which he apologizes, so that ten volumes in all came from his pen. Five are in Edinburgh University Library, one is in the British Museum. These, with the Dublin one, make seven in all. Three parts are still missing—the duplicate tenor, contra-tenor, and fifth part. The contra-tenor is particularly wanted, as the original contra-tenor is incomplete. It is much to be desired that the setting of all the original parts should be reconstructed, that so we might recover the earliest examples of choral singing of the Psalms to be found in Scotland.

The Scottish Reformers, to their credit, did not follow Calvin's example of forbidding such singing: there is nothing on record to show that they regarded it with disfavour. On the contrary, only ten years after the 1564 Psalter appeared, we find evidence of harmonic singing being in use. James Melville records in his *Diary* of 1574, when he was a student in St. Andrews, that 'I learned my music, wherein I tuk graitter delyt, of ane Alexander Smithe, servant to the Primarius of our College, who had been treaned upe amangis the mounks in the Abbay. I learned of him the gam [i.e.

---

[1] This part-book contains 'Songs of four and five parts, meet and apt for musicians to recreate their spirits'.

gamut or scale], plean song, and monie of the treables of the Psalmes, whereof sum I could weill sing in the Kirk.' The 'treable' part, be it noted, was not the melody, which was in the tenor, the 'people's part', but the uppermost part in the score, intended to be sung by women and the unbroken voices of boys. The inference is that in St. Andrews, so early, these high-pitched voices were given their part in the singing in the Kirk.

Eight years later, in 1582, when John Durie, a redoubtable exiled minister, returned to Edinburgh, he was met at the Netherbow Port by a concourse of people who accompanied him on his progress to St. Giles's, increasing as it went to a number estimated at 2,000. Calderwood relates that

'at the Netherbow they took up the 124 Psalme, "Now Israel may say", etc., and sung in such a pleasant tune in four parts, known to the most part of the people, that coming up the street all bareheaded till they entered in the Kirk, with such a great sound and majestie, that it moved both themselves and all the huge multitude of the beholders, looking out at the shots and over stairs with admiration and astonishment: the Duke himself [Lennox] beheld, and reave his beard for anger; he was more affrayed of this sight than anie thing that ever he had seene before in Scotland.'

What these 'four parts' were it is impossible now to say. Wood's part-books may have been roughly copied for current use. It is significant that many of his harmonies reappear in the great Psalter of 1635. But other harmonizations were also available. Dr. H. M. Willsher discovered among the Panmure papers no fewer than forty settings of psalm-tunes, of a high order of merit, by Andro Kemp or Kempt, who was at the Sang Schule of Dundee, then that of St. Andrews, and finally was master of the Sang Schule of Aberdeen from 1570 to 1573.

There is the further possibility that in the crowd there were a number of singers trained in the old Song School of St. Giles's or Trinity College, who had skill enough to sing from memory, or to 'put in' an extemporized bass or alto or treble. It is easy to understand how the impression of four-part singing would be created. But here is definite proof that such singing was then already in common use, at least in centres where the song-schools continued or their tradition persisted.

Chapter 7

The Great Scottish Psalter of 1635

THIS Psalter represents the high-water mark of the psalmody of the Reformation in Scotland. Here the Church music of the period comes to its climax.

The editor conceals his own identity under the initials 'E.M.' But these are now known to stand for Edward Millar, who graduated at Edinburgh University in 1624, and afterwards taught 'bairns' in Blackfriars Wynd.

Like Thomas Wood of the St. Andrews Psalter before him, he is modest in his estimate of his own proficiency in the musical art: in his own phrase he claims no more than 'poor talents', though he has spent 'much time, travail, and expenses' upon what he has tried to do. One of his aims, he says, was to amend certain abuses 'observed in all Churches, where sundrie Tribles, Bases and Counters set by diverse Authors, being sung upon one and the same Tenor [the melody] do discordingly rub each upon another, offending both Musicall and rude ears, which never tasted of this art, which unhappie fault [he] thought might happily bee helped, and the Church Musick made more plausible, by publishing this Booke'. He names a number of the musicians whose help Wood had enlisted fifty years before—John Angus, Andrew Blackhall of Musselburgh, 'Sir' John Black of Aberdeen, John Buchan (see p. 59), Smith and Sharp, of whom no particulars are given, and others, 'the primest Musicians that ever this kingdom had'—whose harmonizations he has made use of. Indeed he says that 'the whole compositions of the parts' belong to them and to 'others famous for their skill in this kind. I would bee most unwilling', he says, 'to wrong such shyning lights of this art, by obscuring their names, and arrogating anything to my selfe, which any wayes might derogate from them.' The settings collected from these men by Wood must have been in circulation in manuscript, and others, like those of Andro Kempt, must also have had some amount of current use. The editor made it his business, he says, to collect all the sets he could find on the Psalms, to select the best, and where the parts 'set down by these skillful Authors have beene wronged and vitiat by unskillful copiers thereof', to correct the errors, and, by thus doing the harmonizers justice, 'approve himself to God in a good conscience'.

Upon this work he must have spent years of preparation. Nine years before 1635 he was already far advanced. A copy of Andro Hart's 1615 Psalter exists which has bound up with it 112 leaves of manuscript music. These contain four-part settings of sixteen common tunes and of seventy-five out of the hundred and five proper tunes. In three of the music staves at the end of Psalm 150 there are clearly written the signature and the date, 'E. Millar, 2 Aprile 1626'.[1] Instead of the usual tune for Psalm 124 there is another, which reappears in 1635 as a second tune to that Psalm

[1] A photograph of the page in question may be seen in William Cowan's invaluable *Bibliography of the Book of Common Order*.

TITLE-PAGE OF THE TENOR PART OF THOMAS WOOD'S
ST. ANDREWS PSALTER, 1562–66

(*See Chapter 6*)

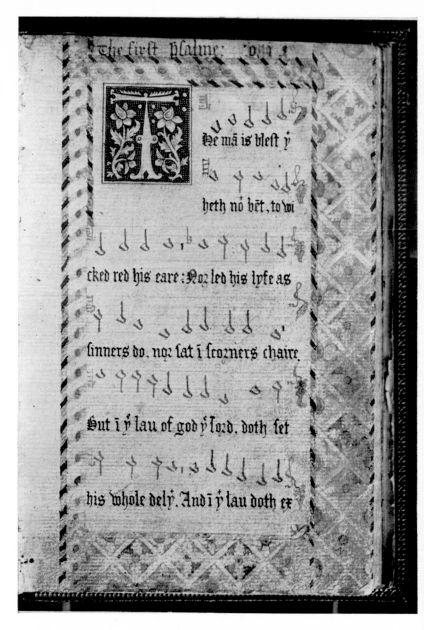

PAGE OF MUSIC FROM THE ST. ANDREWS PSALTER

and is believed to have been Millar's own work. Comparison of these 1626 harmonies with those of 1635 shows that they are almost identical.

In pursuing this difficult and painstaking task throughout so many years Millar's name and repute must have become well known, and it is not surprising that in 1635 Charles I appointed him Master of the Music in the Chapel Royal, because of 'his experience and skill in the art of music'.

Millar proves himself a good editor. He assorts his material under three headings.

I. *The Proper Tunes* naturally occupy the greater part of the book. For they accord with the ideal of the Reformers, which was to give each Psalm its own tune, as indissolubly wedded to it as the air of any well-known secular song is to the words for which it was written. This ideal was not completely realized. In these early Psalters the same tune is sometimes used to two Psalms, despite the general rule that each Psalm should have its own tune and no other.

Millar used a good deal of liberty in editing the tunes. Some that appeared in 1564 disappear altogether; others appear in alliance with different sets of words. The confusion of harmonies which he sought to remedy necessitated modifications of some of the earlier arrangements in Wood's St. Andrews Psalter; the modifications indeed are in many cases so great as to constitute new arrangements.

All the French melodies are retained to the same Psalms, among them Bourgeois's great tunes to Psalms 27, 70, 85, 107, 110, 118, 122, and 134. Two—112 and

F

113—are German chorales, of superlative dignity and splendour; 113 received a second treatment among the Psalms 'in Reports'. Fourteen tunes are taken from the English Psalters. But how many others are English and how many Scottish it is impossible to say, for the great majority are drawn from the Anglo-Genevan books, the tunes in which are anonymous. Some are believed to exhibit traces of the Scottish style, but supposed traces are not conclusive. Anything less than proof is unsafe. The tune PSALM 80, for example, was confidently assumed from its style to be of Scottish origin, until it was discovered in a pre-Reformation source, the *Graduale Altovadense* of 1410.

It must be enough to say that all the harmonies in the 1635 book were by Scottish composers, as were also twenty-four of the Common tunes and all the settings 'in Reports'.

II. *The Common Tunes* compose the first section of the book. The Proper tunes were for singers who could read music. But masses of the Scottish people then could not read at all. Centuries of exclusion from the sung part of public worship made it necessary to make suitable provision to enable them even to begin to sing in the House of God; they had to be helped to acquire the very alphabet of what was to them an unfamiliar art.

First among the tunes in this section is one, called OLD COMMON, upon which the beginners had to make their difficult start. From the fact that it is already called 'Old' in 1615 it may be inferred that it had by that time been long in use. Not improbably it may be

assumed to go back as far as 1550, when the first of the
Sternhold and Hopkins Psalms came to Scotland. They
came without music, and a tune had to be found for
them. What is likelier than that it was this one, with
its unmistakable reminiscence of an older style, and its
requisite simplicity? It must have been learned, as the
words also had to be, 'by ear', and would be widely
used in places where no other tune was known. It is
simple, pathetic; and when it is remembered that great
numbers of the people had their first lesson in it in
how to use their own voices in the music of public
worship, it is very moving in its significance.

THE OLD COMMON TUNE

In 1602 two other tunes of the same order are found
in an edition of the Scottish Psalter published in Middelburg. Both, like OLD COMMON, are as yet without
names. Of English origin—one from Daman's Psalter
of 1579 and the other from Este's of 1592—they came
to be known as LONDON and ENGLISH. Along with
OLD COMMON they constituted the first group of
Common tunes.

It was not till the Psalter of 1615, however, that they
were first classed together under that name. Such a
classification had no precedent elsewhere. The number
included in the group rose to twelve in 1615, and

increased in successive Psalters until in 1635 there were
thirty-one—a clear proof of their growing popularity.
Since they could be used with any Psalm in common
metre, it became necessary to have names to distin-
guish them. Este began the process of naming them in
the English Psalter of 1592. Why particular names were
chosen is quite uncertain, except possibly in the case
of DUNFERMLINE, which is almost certainly the work
of 'good and meike John Angus', one of the conventual
brethren of Dunfermline Abbey, and sometime precentor there, who accepted the Reformation.

Of the Common tunes in the 1635 Psalter, the follow-
ing which are still in use seem, on the evidence avail-
able, to be definitely Scottish: ABBEY, CAITHNESS,
CULROSS, DUKE'S, DUNDEE, DUNFERMLINE, ELGIN,
FRENCH, GLENLUCE, MARTYRS, MELROSE, NEW-
TOUN (LONDON NEW except for the third line), WIG-
TOWN, YORK.

III. The third section of the 1635 Psalter contains a
number of what are called *Tunes in Reports*. This last
word is from the French *rapporter*, to carry back. The
modern word for the usage is 'imitation'. It means the
taking up by a voice or voices of a part of a melodic
phrase just heard from another. Simple examples appear in the tunes BON ACCORD and ABERFELDY (originally MONTROSSE TUNE) which alone of their species
survive from Edward Raban's Aberdeen Psalters of
1625 and 1633. The fugal treatment applied to some of
these tunes turned them into short motets or anthems.
'The psalm tune proceeds in one part (generally the
tenor) with longish rests between the lines of the

poetry, enabling the other voices to enter in imitation, sometimes of a rather vague kind.'[1]

These were obviously departures from the original principle that 'curiosity' of music should be avoided in the treatment of the Psalms. They implied an attempt to revert to the kind of Church music from which the Reformed Church departed. At the time when this took place efforts were being made in high places to undo the Reformers' policy of 'Thorough'. There must have been a race of singers then who had inherited the traditions of the old song-schools, and who regarded with resentful feelings the stripping from the new plain mode of worship of everything which gave scope for their special skill. They welcomed the idea of building motets on the foundation of the simple psalm-tunes, and of doing this with a good deal of elaboration. No words were printed with the music, so that the skilled singers, trained in the difficult art of underlaying the musical notation with the appointed words, might have it all their own way, without any intervention from the unskilled congregation, when the Psalms in question were sung. Doubtless these settings were sung a good deal in private where trained singers consorted. But Dr. Livingston has good ground for believing that they were sung as anthems in the Chapel Royal, where Millar himself was in charge of the music. Since 1617, according to the Privy Seal Records, the English service had been maintained in the Chapel, 'with the singing of choristers, surplices, and playing on organs'.

[1] *The Oxford Companion to Music,* p. 792.

The mode in which the Psalter was printed proves that it was intended for choir use, and as yet there were no choirs except in the Royal Chapel. It is true that the tenor is still called the church part, but it is significant that in some of the pieces the people were discouraged from attempting to sing their part, by alterations introduced into the 'Reports' version of the tune. No guidance is given as to phrasing or expression, lest the secrets of the skilled singers' art should be encroached upon. Special treatment is ventured even in two of the Common tunes—CULROSS and DUNFERMLINE—and in the Mixolydian tone at 62, five parts being given in each, with the quintus in the central position.

In printing the tunes in 1635 the Proper tunes were not set out in score; each part was given separately, the contra first, followed by the tribble and bassus; the tenor or people's part comes last so that it may be nearest the words, and it alone has the first stanza printed below the notes. There is a different arrangement with the Common and Reports tunes. In them the tenor and contra are on one page, and the tribble and bassus are opposite, upside-down, so that four singers in opposite pairs with the book lying between them and three tunes occupying two pages, might sing their several parts from the same book.

According to the custom of the age the melody was assigned to the tenor, that word meaning the part that was *held* (Latin *tenere*), while the other parts, in contra-puntal fashion, sang parallel melodies. The treble and contra were harmonic parts above the tenor in pitch, and presumably were sung, the treble by boys' or female voices, and the contra by low-pitched women's or high-pitched men's voices. While thus the mass of the people sang the tenor or church part, the other parts encompassed the melody with harmony. Each setting is in effect a Faux-Bourdon, except for the two Aberdeen Reports, which have the melody in the top part.

The key-signature was no indication of the pitch at which the tune was to be sung. Clefs were placed so as to help the printer by avoiding leger lines; and to make reading easier the keys were limited to two—C and F; for the others accidentals were used as required.

Considerable use was made of the old ecclesiastical modes. Twenty-one tunes are in the second or Dorian mode—MARTYRS, of course, being one, and ELGIN, to our surprise, another. Six are in the third or Phrygian mode; six in the fifth or Mixolydian; while forty-nine are in the major key, and twenty-two in the minor.

The melodies are characterized by a severe simplicity and dignity, and the same simplicity is exhibited by the harmonies. Care is taken to secure in every part tunefulness of progression, so that each part may have as much melodic interest as possible. Discords are sparingly employed. Common chords are for the most part in fundamental positions. The major third—the beautiful Tierce de Picardie—is invariably found at the close of the minor tunes.

The editor's work was very well done, and is the more creditable because various errors show how well justified was his admirable modesty about his own musical abilities. So eminent an authority on the music of the period as Sir Richard Terry said that this Psalter is 'a highly effective art-work, which compares more than favourably with similar work produced in other countries'. He said further that 'the counterpoints in the Scottish book are not so highly polished, nor do they flow so freely as those in the English Psalters, but they have a rough dignity and grandeur that is all their own'.

Yet this fine Psalter did not have an influence proportionate to its quality. No other edition of the Psalmbook *with music*, except a reprint in 1640 of Hart's 1634 edition, was published before, in 1644, the 1546 Psalter ceased to be printed in any edition at all.

There are problems connected with this Psalter which are difficult to solve. So far as can be discovered there was no authorization by the Church behind its publication. One wonders whether Calderwood's words in connexion with other editions issued without authority should be applied to it: 'This labour was undertaken without direction and approbation of the Kirk.'

Equally mystifying is the fact that Millar does not acknowledge the assistance in his work of any contemporary musician; his admitted indebtednesses are all to the men to whom, seventy years before, Wood owned his debt in the St. Andrews Psalter; these must have been in their graves before Millar's work was done. Apparently his aim must have been to produce a later equivalent to what Wood had tried to do, one based also as far as possible on what Wood had actually accomplished. And there must have been influential support for him, for if the Church was not responsible for his venture the cost of producing so elaborate a work would have been, without liberal financial assistance, a sheer impossibility. As Livingston says, 'It is not likely that the project of providing harmony was formally sanctioned by the Church authorities, but leading men may have given their approval privately.' The approval must have taken a substantial form.

There is the further mystifying fact that a musical work of such high quality should have been issued at a time when it did not represent the musical practice of the Church. For all the facts justify the inference that that practice was on a much lower level. The book can indeed have had but a limited actual use. Millar's supporters are not unlikely to have been those who sympathized with the Stuarts' efforts to raise the standard, as they conceived it, of Scottish worship. If they were, it is not surprising that when these efforts came to their disastrous end, a book for which the Master of the Music in the Chapel Royal had been responsible should have been involved in the general wreck.

What Millar's own fate was, history does not tell. 'How long he survived has not been ascertained.' Nor do we know whether he spent his latest days in the quiet living to which King Charles had presented him in 1634, of 'the Kirk and parochine of Sanct Marie Kirk of the Lowis, lyand in Atrick Forrest'. But his work entitles him to honour, alike by the persistence with which he pursued his ideal through the labours of many years, and by the highly meritorious conclusion to which he brought it.

The value of the work, and the credit of the modest

man to whom we owe it, might never have been appreciated had not the Rev. Neil Livingston, of the Free Church of Stair in Ayrshire, found a copy, studied it with eager interest, and been enabled by the munificence of a Glasgow merchant and musical enthusiast, William Euing, to publish a reprint of it, equipped with Dissertations and Appendixes exhibiting an extraordinary range, depth, and thoroughness of scholarship. His great book fell almost dead from the press in 1864. There was a time when a copy might be picked up for sixpence. But it is now recognized as in its own field an editorial master-work, upon whose fullness and accuracy of information every subsequent student of psalmody must depend.

A copy of it fell into the hands of Sir Richard Runciman Terry, Mus.D., Master of the Music in Westminster Roman Catholic Cathedral,[1] London. His excitement over the discovery was unbounded. First he wrote an enthusiastic but discriminating article on it, *A Forgotten Psalter*[2] (1929); then published a photographic reproduction of Livingston's reprint of the music of the Psalter (1935)[3] 'edited with modal harmonies'. This book is valuable; but, for reasons not difficult to understand, the inexhaustibly rich Dissertations and Appendixes were omitted. Terry had no quarrel with them on the score of inaccuracy.

[1] When the Tercentenary of this Psalter was celebrated by a special service and recital in St. Giles's Cathedral, Edinburgh, Sir Richard travelled up from London to attend it.

[2] Published in *A Forgotten Psalter and other Essays* (Oxford University Press).

[3] Published by Novello & Company, Limited.

'In the circumstances [of the limited sources of information in Livingston's day] it is remarkable,' he says, 'how little his Dissertations need in the way of correction. On the subject of the ecclesiastical Modes, for example, he is rarely wrong—which is more than can be said of many Plainsong "experts" of to-day. ... He left behind him a work of high value, and every musician is now his debtor.'

III

The Second
Scottish
Psalter
1650

Chapter 8

The Genesis of the Second (1650) Psalter

THE 1564 Psalter cannot at any time have had more than a very restricted use. On the literary side it was open to extremely damaging criticism, though we get no proper measure of contemporary judgement of it by applying to it the standards of the present day. But the metres used were too various, and many of the versions were far from being simple enough to make memorizing easy for a people who were still, in the mass, unable to read. The music, too, was more than the people could learn. Francis Rous, in the preface to the 1646 edition of his own version, justifying the use of measures 'fitted to such tunes as have been found by experience to be of most generall use', says:

'True it is, that in a former edition Psalms have been set forth in measures fitted for more difficult tunes, which are still to be seen; but it was objected by very good judgements, that if such difficult tunes were allowed, some man willing to make use (if not shew) of his skill, might begin a Psalm in a tune wherein the Congregation might be put to a losse. For they might either not follow him at all or follow him in a discord, instead of a harmony. And indeed it is very suitable to charity, that those that have skill should condescend to them that have none, and not by that skill hinder edification of the unskillful.'

Here we have the distillation of much experience of the

English Psalter. For Scotland, also, its first Psalter was too far ahead of the capacity of the people.

It is true that the author—supposed to be Calderwood the historian—of a scathing array of arguments against the public use of King James's 'Metaphrase' of the Psalms, used this among his objections: 'The people ar well acquanted with the old metaphrase [the 1564 one] more than any book in scripture, zea, some can sing all, or the most pairt without buik, and some that can not read can sing some psalmes.' He says further:

'Both pastors and people be long custome, ar so acquanted with the psalmes and tunes thereof; that as the pastors ar able to direct a psalme to be sung agrieable to the doctrine to be delyvered, so he that taketh up the psalme is able to sing anie tune, and the people for the most pairt to follow him. Both people and pastors have some psalmes, or parts of psalmes, be heart, as may best serve for their different disposition and ease of conscience, and for the chainges of ther externall condition. By the loss of that heavenly treasure in ther hart alreadie, they would be farder greived, and prejudged in ther spirituall estate than they could be hurt in bodie or goodes suffering for retention of ther own psalmes.'

This was in 1631.

It should be remembered, however, that this was written in an endeavour to make the best of a doubtful case, in order to countervail a determined effort to impose an entirely obnoxious alternative version—alleged to be King James's—upon an unwilling Church. The weight of the assertions as to the extent to which the existing Psalter had hold upon the people's minds is much diminished by the incontrovertible fact that by the time when the new version of 1650 was ready, psalm-singing was in a very bad way in Scotland, and indeed, within the metropolitan area, had ceased. It is significant, also, that, so far as is known, not a single word of regret was recorded when the old version was dismissed from use.

Dissatisfaction with the 1564 version would probably have come to a head more quickly if King James had not barred the way to an impartial consideration of any attempt to provide an alternative to his own. In 1591 a work was published entitled *His Majesties Poeticall Exercises at Vacant Hours,* in the preface to which he thus addressed the reader: 'Rough and unpolished as they are I offer them unto thee: which being well accepted, will move me to haste the presenting unto thee of my Apocalyps, and also *such nomber of the Psalmes as I have perfited, and encourage me to the ending out of the rest.*'

Apparently the encouragement was given him, for he made himself thenceforward the chief sponsor of a better version. At the General Assembly held at Burntisland in 1601, a proposal having been made to have a new translation of the Bible and a revisal of the Psalms in metre,

'King James did urge very earnestly, and with many reasons did persuade the undertaking of the work, shewing the necessity and the profit of it and what a glory the performing of it should bring to this church: ... and when he came to speak of the Psalms he did recite whole verses of the same, shewing both the faults of the metre and the discrepance from the text. It was the joy of all present to hear it, and bred not little admiration in the whole assembly.'

G

Cautiously, the admiring Assembly refrained from any immediate action beyond that of falling back on one of its safest and most trusted counsellors, Robert Pont. To placate the kingly critic it ordained that Pont 'sould revise the psalmes, and that his labours sould be revised at the next assemblie'; and the record ran that as the motion which led to his receiving this commission

'proceeded from personall respects, so it is to be supposed, that if that faithfull man, who was both holy and learned, had found anie just cause of alteration, nether he to whom the mater was recommended nor the assemblie who should have taken compt of his diligence, would have suffered that mater to be buried in oblivion.'

That, however, was exactly the course which both Pont and the Assembly deemed the proper one to follow: they did nothing, in the hope that the whole affair would be forgotten. Unfortunately, James was the last man to forget. If the Assembly would not act, he himself would. 'The good-natured, conceited, garrulous King, wise in learning, but a poor judge of men', to borrow G. M. Trevelyan's characterization of him,[1] in nothing showed his conceit more ridiculously than in thinking himself the man to show the way to the production of a more poetical version. He set to work upon this ambitious effort. 'The revising of the Psalmes he made his own labour, and at such hours as he might spare from public cares, went through a number of them, commending the rest to a faithful and

---

[1] *History of England*, p. 381.

learned servant, who hath therein answered his Majesty's expectation.'

This known ambition of the King cleared the field of overt competition. Many other writers were working privately at versions of their own. Calderwood says that Alexander Montgomerie (*c.* 1545–*c.* 1610), the author of *The Cherrie and the Slae*, and others, 'principalls of English poesie in ther tymes, as they gave their assayes of som psalmes yet extant, so they offered to translate the whole booke frielie without anie pryce for their paines, ether frae the public state or privat mens purses'. Sir William Mure of Rowallan (d. 1652), that greatly gifted man, classical scholar, poet, musician, compiler of the *Rowallan Lute Book* (1612–28), and withal, from first to last a deeply religious man and a staunch Covenanter, exercised his talents on a new version of the Psalms. So did Drummond of Hawthornden (1585–1649). Writing to him, Sir William Alexander of Menstrie (*c.* 1567–1640), afterwards Secretary of State for Scotland and latterly Earl of Stirling, said:

'Brother, I received your last letter, with the Psalm you sent, which I think very well done. I had done the same long before it came; but He [King James] prefers his own to all else; tho' perchance when you see it, you will think it the worst of the Three. No man must meddle with that Subject, and therefore I advise you to take no more Pains therein.'

During James's lifetime his design was successfully baulked. A serious situation arose, however, when Charles succeeded to the throne. 'He had no sense of the possible, nor any understanding of the Scots.'[1]

---

[1] Wallace Notestein, *The Scot in History*, p. 142.

But he was nothing if not a loyal son, and he made it a matter of filial duty to see his father's purpose carried into effect. He instructed Alexander 'to consider and revew the meeter and poesie' of the royal version, and, whatever his private opinion might be, Alexander, as a loyal courtier, had no option but to obey.

From the funeral sermon preached on King James's death by the Bishop of Lincoln—a sermon entitled 'Great Britain's Salomon'—we learn how far James himself had gone in his enterprise. After declaring that in the late King was 'observed all that was admirable in the eloquence of Salomon', the Bishop went on:

'For, beside his prose, *Iter ad carmen nouerat,* hee made a verse also when he pleas'd, and that (as became Buchanan's best scholler) *sanissimi coloris,* of a most dainty and elaborate composition. An everlasting honour to the Muses! . . . So the greatest potentate of all the Earth may now stoop to a Verse, being the usuall Recreation of King David, together with this first and second Salomon. The King our Master, was in hand (when God called him to sing Psalmes with the Angels) with the translation of our Church Psalmes, which he intended to have finished, and dedicated withall to the onely saint of his devotion, the Church of Great Britain, and that of Ireland. The worke was staied in the one and thirty Psalme.'

As a single specimen of James's handiwork Psalm I is here given from a volume of Psalms 'in the Scottish dialect, written in his Majesty's own hand', preserved in the British Museum:

    1. That mortal man most happy is and blest
       Who in the wickeds counsals doth not walk,
       Nor zit in sinners wayis doth stay and rest,
       Nor sittis in seatis of skornful men in talk,

2. But contrair fixis his delicht
     Into Jehouas law
     And on his law, both day and nicht,
     To think is neuer slaw.

3. He salbe lyk a plesant plantit tree,
     Vpon a reuer syde incressing tal,
     That yieldis his fruit in saison dew, we see,
     Whose plesant leif doth neuer fade nor fal.
          Now this is surely for to say
          That quhat he takis in hand,
          It sal withoutin doute alway
          Most prosperously stand.

4. Bot wickit men ar nowayis of that band;
     But as the caffe quhich be the wind is tost:
5. Thairfor they sall not in the iugement stand
     Nor yett among the iust be sinneris lost.
          6. For gret Jehoua cleirly knowis
          The iust mens way vpricht,
          But sure the wickeds way that throwis
          Sall perish be his micht.

Sir William Alexander fulfilled the commission given
him by King Charles in August 1626. Archbishop
Spottiswoode of St. Andrews was instructed to examine what he produced, with the assistance of other
learned Divines, and to certify the fidelity of it to the
original text. Like good courtiers, these Divines found
themselves able to say that it was 'exactly and truely
done, and fit to be sung in all the churches of the three
Kingdoms'.

Thereupon, in 1631, the version submitted by
Alexander was printed at Oxford under the title: *The
Psalmes of King David translated by King James*. The

title-page bore a device representing King David on one side with a harp, and King James on the other with his sceptre, and both holding a book. On another page the royal arms appear with King Charles's authorization of what he describes as 'this Translation of the Psalmes (whereof our late deare Father was Author)'. This attribution of authorship was known even then to be false: the version was commonly called 'the Menstrie Psalms'. Let the first Psalm as printed in it be compared with King James's own version given above, and the justice of this description will be realized.

1. The man is blest that doth not walke
   where wicked councells guide;
   Nor in the way of sinners stands,
   nor scorners sits beside:
2. But of the Lord he on the law
   doth ground his whole delight;
   And on his law doth meditate
   devoutly day and night.

3. He shall be like a planted tree,
   the streames of water neare;
   Whose pleasant boughs bring timely fruit
   in season of the yeare.
4. His leafe it never wither shall
   as Winters blasted prey:
   And whatsoever he designes
   shall prosper every way.

5. But wicked men are nothing so,
   for they as chaffe shall prove;
   Which whirling windes doe drive away
   and from the earth remove.

6. They who are wickedly dispos'd,
   no such assurance finde:
   But like unto contemned chaffe,
   are tossed with the winde.

The 1631 edition was not enforced: the King restricted
himself to saying, we 'doe allow them to be sung in all
the Churches of oure Dominiones, recommending
them to all our good Subjects for that effect'. But
indignation seethed in many breasts, and did not lack
expression. A formidable barrage of reasons against the
public use of James's 'Metaphrase' is preserved in a
volume of manuscripts collected by David Calderwood, and is believed to have been written by none
other than himself. It numbers among the objections
to the *public* use of it the 'heathenish libertie and
poeticall conceats' employed, 'harsh phrases', 'words
which have need of a dictionarie', of which many
specimens are given, and the risk that it might 'mak
uther Kirkis call vs lightheaded Scotts, inconstant and
vnsettled in our orders, changing without anie neces-
sitie'. Among the reasons alleged against the *private*
use of the Metaphrase is the fact that 'another metaphrase is nevir convenient, bot prejudiciall to that
which is used in the Kirk and serveth onlie to mak
people glaik'.

Charles's answer to the opposition was to enjoin the
Privy Council of Scotland, in December 1634, to give
orders that 'no other Psalmes of any edition whatsoever
be either printed heirafter within that our Kingdome,
or imported thither, either bound by themself or
otherways from any forraigne parts'. But two years

later, in 1636, the Oxford edition of the offending version was succeeded by another, published in London, so thoroughly revised and altered as to amount to an entirely new version, but without any intimation that such thorough-going revision had taken place.

In spite of the royal edict, Charles's wish that what was alleged to be King James's work should be 'a perpetual monument to the memory of his beloved father' was not to be gratified. The Archbishop of Canterbury (Laud) took no effective steps to impose the new Psalter on England: he was sufficiently embroiled in other and graver troubles to realize the wisdom of shirking this new one. His Grace of St. Andrews, more complaisant, instructed his clergy to obtemper the King's instruction, but sensibly did nothing further. The Presbyteries, consulted, recognized that inaction was the proper strategy: as Row says, 'that matter was laid asyde for a while'.

Portentous events were now rapidly following one another. In February 1638 the National Covenant was signed in Greyfriars Church. In September a Royal Proclamation revoked the Scottish Service-book and summoned meetings of a free General Assembly and a free Parliament; and in November the Glasgow Assembly 'swept away the whole ecclesiastical edifice which had been reared [in Scotland] with such expenditure of time and pains by Charles and his father'. In that summary clearance, the Liturgy and the Royal Psalter which was bound up with it were decisively banished from use[1] and honour in the Church of Scot-

---

[1] Apparently the Psalter had actually been to some extent in use. In

land. In England also the situation was steadily worsening for the King and his designs. In 1640 Laud was sent to the Tower, Strafford was impeached and in May 1641 was executed; the Long Parliament was in session, and the wreck of the royal system was begun.

the Reasons against it already referred to this occurs: 'For have not some alreadie vsed this metaphrase when the congregation were singing the old? A door should not be opened to such light heads and prophane hearts.'

Chapter 9

Francis Rous and the Scottish Psalter

So long as King James's venture as psalmodist seemed to have first claim to the right of way, any attempt to bring another version into the field would have looked almost like *lèse-majesté*. Other adventurers, however, were but awaiting their opportunity. Among them was Francis Rous. He was a scholar and a gentleman, an influential member of the Puritan party in England, and Provost of Eton College. His political importance may be measured by the fact that he became Speaker of the Barebones Parliament, a member of Cromwell's Council of State, and, in 1657, a peer of the realm. He had prepared a version of the Psalms, and had it in readiness when, in 1638, it became evident that the Royal Psalter had no chance of acceptance anywhere, and that an acceptable alternative would have to be found.

Taking time by the forelock, he manœuvred to get his version into a commanding position as against any rival, by securing parliamentary sanction for it as soon as the way was clear. He had it printed without his name, in Rotterdam, and brought over to England for distribution—not, it is surmised, indiscriminately, but only among members of Parliament. In 1640 he saw that his opportunity had come. He published his second edition in London in 1641, with his name on

the title-page, and intensified his efforts to get parliamentary sanction for it. His prospects of success were
good. His own influence with the Commons was great,
and his friends were assiduous in lobbying for him.
There is no reason to question his own disinterested-
ness, but Baillie[1] says that one consideration with which
his supporters made effective play was 'the great
private advantage which could by this book come to
their friend'. Many in the House were not impressed;
they thought the work not done well enough to deserve support. But Rous's supporters prevailed over
the opposition, and in April 1643 the Committee on
Printing was instructed to print his book for general
use.

That act, however, was far from final. In June the
Assembly of Divines, convened by 'ordinance' of both
Houses of Parliament, met at Westminster to devise
ways and means of securing uniformity of church
doctrine, discipline, organization and worship throughout the three kingdoms; and in November the Commons requested it to advise whether it might not be
useful and profitable to the Church that Rous's book
should be issued, with an injunction that its contents
should be publicly sung throughout the land. The
Assembly, however, refused to be rushed into any
hasty decision. It referred the book for examination to
three Committees, each of which was instructed to
revise fifty of the Psalms. They conferred with Rous
himself. One of them was anxious that a select Com-

[1] Robert Baillie's Letters are the chief source of our knowledge of this
part of the story.

mittee of 'Hebricians' should be called into council, to ensure the 'solidity' of the work, but the idea was not acted upon. Next, it was resolved that the whole version, as revised, should be read openly in the full Assembly, no debate to be then allowed, but suggestions of amendment to be afterwards sent to the Committee.

Among the Commissioners to the Assembly, those from Scotland were the most difficult to satisfy. They were a remarkable group: Alexander Henderson, Robert Douglas (never sat), Samuel Rutherford, Robert Baillie, George Gillespie, and (later, but probably never sat) Robert Blair, *ministers*; and John, Earl of Cassillis (never sat), John, Lord Maitland, afterwards Earl of Lauderdale, Sir Archibald Johnston of Warriston, and (later) John, Earl of Loudon, Sir Charles Erskine, John, Lord Balmerino, Archibald, Marquis of Argyle, and George Winram of Libberton, *elders*. They were strongly in favour of uniformity, and agreed that a common Psalter would be an almost essential contribution towards that end; but they exhibited native caution in their attitude to the new version proposed for this honour. They insisted that the Kirk of Scotland should be 'well advised' as to what was happening, and saw that Rous's Psalms, as revised by the Assembly, were sent north in instalments to receive what they called 'animadversions'. 'We earnestlie intreat you', they wrote, 'to mind seriouslie the review of them, what words or lines you think ought to be amended', and expressed anxiety that 'the Psalter might at this time be put in such a frame that we need not be troubled hereafter with any new translation thereof'. We can sympathize with that anxiety. 'These lines', wrote Baillie, 'are likely to go up to God from millions of tongues for many generations: it were a pity but all possible diligence were used to have them framed so well as might be.'

Individuals like Mure of Rowallan and Zachary Boyd, both authors of versions of their own, were appealed to for assistance; but the chief work of revision was done by Committees of the Church. It is unfortunate that the Minutes of the Committee of the Commission of Assembly between 1643 and 1646 are lost, so that details of the procedure followed are unknown; but it is clear that the opportunity given was fully taken advantage of. Many animadversions by the Scottish critics were sent up to Westminster. These were favourably received, and almost all of them were followed; Mr. Rous himself, says Baillie, and all the Committee proved very tractable. So the matter moved to a conclusion. At last, on 25 November 1645, Baillie writes: 'The Psalmes are perfyted; the best without doubt that ever yet were extant.'

Observe then what had happened. Rous's version had undergone drastic alteration, first at the hands of the Westminster Assembly, then at those of the Kirk of Scotland. The result was so great a change in it that Rous ceased to make any claim to authorship. His preface disappeared; inevitably so, for the version that emerged from the hands of the Divines was very different from that for which it had been written. Though his name continued to be used in connexion with it, such a use is inaccurate: the new version ought to be distinguished from his by being called the Westminster Version.

What then was *its* fate? Its difficulties did not end when the Assembly of Divines set their imprimatur upon it. It had still to run the gauntlet of both Houses of Parliament. Its course there was far from easy. Some people demanded 'a libertie to take what psalter they will'. The ministers of London preferred the version of William Barton (*c.* 1603–78), first published anonymously in 1644, but issued with additions and alterations, and printed by order of Parliament in 1645. In the course of a somewhat grandiloquent preface Barton says:

'Touching the translation itself, since Hebrew must be into English, English must be made verse, and verse ryme, wee must of necessity admit some alteration and amplification of words, although without extravagant excursions of unnecessary paraphrase or as frothy flourishes of undivine poetry. But since poetry is a gift of God too, and very notable to kindle, quicken and enflame affection; since this gift in the greatest measure is most necessary for such a work as this wherein such majestie and gracefulness together with plainnes, sweetnes, clearnes (sutable to the capacities of vulgar people, and even of so many women) is required: Methinks none should be of that mind to tie us strictly to the prose and text as must constrain us to render it in such rugged, ingratefull, and misshapen verse, as many judicious men have already much misliked, and such as multitudes of plain people would deem to have neither ryme nor reason.'

In spite of this prologue, Barton's versions were in no way superior to those of the old Reformation Psalmbook, and in all his multiplied adventures in this field (for he left no fewer than 300 psalm-versions different from those in his Psalm-book), there is nothing fit to stand beside the best versions of Sternhold, Whittingham, or Kethe; nor is he to be compared as a poet with his rivals, Wither or Sandys. Yet he was the choice of the London ministers, on the ground that his version was more poetical, and the House of Lords asked the Assembly of Divines to certify why Barton's Psalms should not be sung in churches, as well as other translations, by such as wanted to use them. That liberty, if granted, would of course have ended all hope of uniformity. The result was a deadlock. The Lords never approved the Westminster Version. The Commons refused to countenance Barton.

Baillie throws a little light on the difficulties that delayed proceedings. 'The too great accuracy of some in the Assembly, sticking too hard to the original text, made the last edition more concise and obscure than the former. With this the Commission of our Church was not so well pleased; but we have got all these obscurities helped; so I think it shall pass.' Apparently, also, Zachary Boyd caused trouble by his efforts to get his own version preferred. 'Our good friend Zachary Boyd', says Baillie in the same letter, 'has put himself to a great deal of pains and charges to make a psalter, but I ever warned him his hopes were groundless to get it received in our churches: yet the flatteries of his unadvised neighbours makes him insist in his fruitless design.'

Probably the strain between the two Houses of Parliament was aggravated, if not caused, by the growing jealousy with which the Lords were watching the assumption of leadership by the Commons. In this case the conflict of opinion was ended by the Lower House taking independent action. On 15 April 1646 it ordered that the Westminster version should be printed, and that after 1 January following, 'no other version should be sung in all Churches and Chapels within the Kingdom of England, Dominion of Wales, and Toune of Berwick-upon-Tweede'.

This bold action, however, proved nugatory. The reception of the new version south of the Border was uniformly unfavourable: there is no evidence that it displaced the old one anywhere. One reason for its unpopularity is said to have been the extent to which the Scots had pressed their animadversions and so set too distinctive a Scottish mark upon it.

From this it might have been expected that north of the Border a cordial welcome would await it. The contrary proved to be the case. The Commissioners who had represented the Kirk at Westminster did their best for it. They assured their countrymen that the new translation would be 'found as neir the originall as any paraphrase in meeter can readily be, and much nearer than other works of that kynd; which is', they added, 'a good compensation to make up the want of that poeticall liberty and sweet pleasant running which some desire'. But they failed to carry conviction, and the death-blow to all hopes of Scottish acceptance was dealt when the General Assembly flatly refused to receive the version as a symbol of Presbyterian uniformity, and resolved to submit it to further revision.

Thus the movement was farther and farther away from Rous's original version.

The Assembly used no half-measures in the steps they took. The thoroughgoing way in which they proceeded was typically Scottish. Actually, there were six several revisions before the final result was reached, and the time spent in the process extended to two years and four months.

First: on 8 July 1647, the Assembly 'recommended to Mr. John Adamson to revise Rous's Paraphrase of the Psalms, and Mr. John Row's observations thereupon, and to have his opinion thereof ready for the next Assembly'.

Second: the Assembly met on 28 August in the same year, and appointed a Committee consisting of four interesting and influential men to prosecute the work more thoroughly. The most prominent was John Adamson, just named, who was Principal of the University of Edinburgh. The others were: Thomas Crawford, Professor of Mathematics and Regent in Philosophy in the same University; John Row, named above, who was second son of the historian, minister of St. Nicholas, Aberdeen, and subsequently Principal first of Marischal College and University, then of King's, in that city; and John Nevay, an extremist in his views, who was ultimately banished to Holland and died there. Adamson was instructed to deal with the first group of forty psalms, Crawford was assigned the next forty, Row the third, and Nevay the last thirty.[1] The instruc-

[1] Though Nevay's allotment was the smallest, he drew more largely than any of his colleagues upon the old version. To him also we owe the inclusion of Craig's three second versions, albeit there was little chance of their being sung, for by this time only the Common Tunes were in use,

H

tions given them were: (1) not only to observe what they thought needed to be amended, but also 'to set down their own essay for correcting thereof'; (2) to make use of the 'travels' (travails) of Mure of Rowallan, Zachary Boyd,[1] or any other, and to have special regard to the old version, appropriating whatever they found that was better in any of these; and (3) to make use of the animadversions sent from Presbyteries. The Committee interpreted in the largest sense the instruction to consult and borrow from other existing versions. Internal evidence shows that they drew upon, at the least, ten other versions besides the old Scottish one and the one from Westminster.

Third: in April 1648 they reported to the Commission of Assembly. The ministers of Edinburgh, or any three of them, were thereupon appointed to revise the work of these revisers. It looks as if they had proved either reluctant or dilatory, for, six days later, another Committee of seven was appointed in their place. What happened to dissatisfy the Commission with that Committee does not appear, but only eleven days afterwards, still another, of six members, was appointed to revise further what had been done, and to report their opinion.

Fourth: on 12 July the Assembly met, received the report, and instructed that the revised version should

and Psalms not in Common Metre—even the 100th and the 124th—fell out of use for over a hundred years.

[1] When the work was completed and approved, the Commission of Assembly returned their 'heartie thanks' to Principal Adamson, Zachary Boyd, and Robert Lourie, afterwards Dean of Edinburgh and Bishop of Brechin, for their useful 'travels' while the work was proceeding.

be sent down to Presbyteries for their study and emendations. Not till January of the following year were the copies for this purpose (costing 'a merk the peece', the record says) sent down. The Presbyteries duly exercised diligence in the matter, and in June 1649 the copies with their suggestions returned by them were remitted to Adamson for his consideration against the next meeting of the Assembly. Presumably, all he had to do was to co-ordinate the returns, and prepare a report upon them.

Fifth: when the Assembly met, in August, they remitted Adamson's report to a new Committee of six members, with instructions to report *their* 'travels' to the next following Commission.

Sixth: in November 1649 the Commission met and spent five of its diets on the work of still further revision.

On the 23rd they concluded that task, and, as power had been given them to proceed to publication, they pronounced a deliverance approving of the version as now revised and appointing it to be printed for public use: 'Hereby authorizing the same to be the only Paraphrase of the Psalmes of David to be sung in the Kirk of Scotland: and discharging the old Paraphrase and any other than this new Paraphrase to be made use of in any congregation or family after the first day of May in the year 1650.'

On 8 January 1650 the Committee of Estates, on their part as the civil authority, approved and authorized this course.

Thus the version of the Psalms which has for three

hundred years been the authorized Metrical Psalter of the Church of Scotland came into use on 1 May 1650 bearing the title: *The Psalms of David in Meeter: Newly translated, and diligently compared with the originall Text, and former Translations: More plaine, smooth and agreeable to the Text, than any heretofore.*

In respect of variety of metre the Scottish revisers did not adhere so rigidly as the English to the monotony of Common Metre. In the English book 143 out of the 150 Psalms are in Common Metre: of the remaining seven, four are in Short and three in Long Metre. In the Scottish book the number of versions in other than Common Metre was thirteen. Of these, some were from the Reformation Psalter, called in the Act of Assembly authorizing the book 'our own Paraphrase'. Of these the most notable are the second versions of the 100th by Kethe, the 124th by Whittingham, and the 136th and 145th by Craig. From George Wither the fine second version of Psalm 148 was taken; and the long-metre version of the 102nd is largely founded on Barton's version of that Psalm.

Where now does Rous stand in relation to this version? One radical revision of his version was carried out, with active Scottish participation, at Westminster, leaving only fragments of his work remaining. And on the resultant Westminster version, six separate Scottish revisions were carried out before the work was done. From this the inference is inevitable that not much of Rous would be left in the final version which received the authorization of the Scottish General Assembly. Such an inference would be justified.

Take a concrete example. Compare with the authorized version of Psalm 1 (in the 1650 Psalter) Rous's final form, of 1646.

That man hath perfect blessedness
  who walketh not astray
In counsel of ungodly men,
  nor stands in sinners' way,
Nor sitteth in the scorner's chair:
  but placeth his delight
Upon God's law, and meditates
  on his law day and night.

He shall be like a tree that grows
  near planted by a river,
Which in his season yields his fruit,
  and his leaf fadeth never:
And all he doth shall prosper well.
  The wicked are not so;
But like they are unto the chaff,
  which wind drives to and fro.

In judgment therefore shall not stand
  such as ungodly are;
Nor in th' assembly of the just
  shall wicked men appear.
For why? the way of godly men
  unto the Lord is known:
Whereas the way of wicked men
  shall quite be overthrown.

The man is blest that in th' advice
  of those that wicked are
Walks not, nor stands in sinner's path,
  nor sits in scorner's chaire,
But in God's law delights, on's law
  both day and night doth think;
He shall be like unto a tree
  set by the river's brink,

Whose fruit's in season, leaf fades not:
  all that he doth shall thrive:
Not so the wicked; but like chaffe
  which wind away doth drive.
In judgment therefore wicked men
  shall not stand justify'd;
Nor in the assembly of the just,
  the sinners shall abide.

Because the way of righteous men
  the Lord with favour knowes,
Whereas the way of wicked men
  unto destruction goes.

Only two lines of Rous, it will be observed, are preserved in the Scottish version. As to the merits of the two versions there cannot be two opinions.

Apply another test. The late Dr. W. P. Rorison of Dalserf,[1] with incredible patience and particularity, carried out a detailed comparison of the 1650 version with ten others, in order to trace every line, so far as

[1] A typescript copy of his work, *The Story of the Scottish Psalter,* may be consulted in the Assembly Library, Edinburgh.

might be possible, to its source. There are 8,620 lines in all in the Scottish version. Of these, Dr. Rorison traced the following to their sources:

		lines
Old (1564) version	. . . .	338
Henry Dod (1620)	. . . .	266
King James (1631–6)	. . . .	516
George Wither (1632)	. . . .	52
Mure of Rowallan .	. . . .	49
The Bay Psalter (1640)[1] .	. . .	269
William Barton (1644)[2] .	. . .	136
Zachary Boyd (1644–8) .	. . .	754
Westminster version (1647)	. . .	1,588
Francis Rous (1638–46) .	. . .	878
		4,846

This list of sources is not exhaustive. There is evidence that the revisers had before them, and used, the versions of George Sandys (1636) and Richard Brathwaite (1638), but the extent to which they drew from these has not been examined in detail.

It will be observed that 3,774 lines are not accounted for—nearly half the whole. These may be taken to represent in a large degree the 'travels' of the various companies of Scottish revisers. Yet a distinguished professor of Scottish history is found saying categorically that 'the version of the Psalms, intertwined with the most sacred feelings of the Scottish people . . . came from the Westminster Assembly'.[3] Dr. H. G. Farmer,

[1]   *The Bay Psalter,* later called *The New England Version of the Psalms* (1640), was the first book printed in New England.

[2]   Though Barton was relatively so little drawn upon, he complained bitterly of 'the piracies committed by the Scots'.

[3]   Professor Hume Brown.

in his *History of Scottish Music*, consistently speaks of *Rous's Psalms*.[1]

The following indication of the sources of the 23rd Psalm will illustrate at once how little the version owes to Rous, and how much of a mosaic in reality it is.

The Lord's my shepherd, I'll not want.	*Boyd*
He makes me down to lie	*Rous*
In pastures green: he leadeth me	*Boyd (modified)*
the quiet waters by.	"
My soul he doth restore again;	*Westminster*
and me to walk doth make	"
Within the paths of righteousness,	" *(mod.)*
ev'n for his own name's sake.	*Whittingham (Old Version)*
Yea, though I walk in death's dark vale,	*Westminster*
yet will I fear none ill:	*Sternhold*
For thou art with me; and thy rod	*Westminster (mod.)*
and staff me comfort still.	*Mure*
My table thou hast furnished	*Westminster*
in presence of my foes;	*Mure*
My head thou dost with oil anoint,	*Westminster (mod.)*
and my cup overflows.	*Mure*
Goodness and mercy all my life	*Boyd*
shall surely follow me:	*King James*
And in God's house for evermore	*Westminster*
my dwelling-place shall be.	*Sternhold*

Conclusive evidence has been given of the composite nature of the 1650 Psalter. Dr. Rorison quotes with approval a description of it as 'the Prince of Versions', holding that it deserves this primacy because 'it contains the cream of all the best Psalters in existence

---

[1] It is curious that the Assembly and Commission of Assembly of 1650, in their references to this version, themselves speak of 'Rous's Paraphrase of the Psalmes'.

prior to 1650'. With this we may or may not agree; but at least we may hold it proved beyond controversy that to ascribe it either to Rous or to Westminster is completely unjustified. It is the product in the main of prolonged and devoted Scottish labour, and bears deeply upon it the imprint of Scottish care and piety. It is fully entitled to the distinctive name by which it is commonly known, 'The *Scottish* Psalter'.

The virtues which have endeared it to the Scottish people were well summed up by Dr. John Ker in the volume published after his death, *The Psalms in History and Biography*. After noting some of its admitted imperfections, he says:

'No version has ever been made which adheres so closely to the Scripture. It proceeds on the principle of giving every thought in the original, and nothing more; and in this it has succeeded to an extent which is marvellous, and which can be realised only by one who has tested it through careful comparison. It meets with some stones of stumbling, and suffers some dislocation of words by adhering to the line laid down; but there is abundant compensation in the life and energy, the picturesqueness and colour, which it preserves by close contact with the old Hebrew soil. The thought stands out clear, distinct, forceful, not wrapt up in wordy paraphrases where David himself would have had difficulty in recognising his meaning, or liquefied into weak sentimentalisms from which his manly nature, to take no higher view, would have turned away ashamed. This too may be said, that those portions which the heart feels that it needs in its sorrowful hours, over which it leans and pores in its deep musings, or from the summits of which it mounts as on eagles' wings in its moments of joy, have a tenderness, a quaint beauty, a majesty in their form, peculiar to that age of the English language in which they were framed.'

Chapter 10

The Great Eclipse

WHEN the 1650 Psalter came into use, no music was published with it. This was a breach with the Reformation practice, which was to issue no psalm-book without tunes. It is usual to conclude that the failure to maintain the tradition was a startling measure of public apathy or official indifference. Either, it is supposed, there was nobody in the Church with sufficient interest to see that even the barest minimum of tunes was provided, or there was no force of public opinion to compel those to whom the responsibility belonged to make good the omission.

But such a conclusion does injustice to all concerned. For when inquiry is made into the political, cultural, and religious conditions of the time, what astonishes is not the failure to publish tunes, but the fact that it was found possible to issue any Psalter at all.

For years the country had been distracted by political commotions. The end of the Civil War and the removal of Charles I had brought no relief. Charles II was proclaimed king by the Estates at Edinburgh six days after his father's death. Such a defiance of the dominant party in England could not be disregarded, and in May of the following year (1650)—the very month in which the new Psalter appeared—Cromwell crossed the Tweed to enforce his own solution of the issue confronting the nation. He found the countryside deserted by the people, and the means of feeding his army either carried out of his reach or destroyed. Four months of marching and counter-marching ensued, until the battle of Dunbar, made decisive by the incredibly foolish tactics of the Scots, gave the victory into the invaders' hands. On 7 September Cromwell entered Edinburgh. His troops were at first quartered at Holyrood; then, after fire had largely destroyed the Palace, they were lodged in the churches of the city. There, they stripped the buildings of their furniture and woodwork, to provide fires to keep them warm in the cold of a northern winter.

Cromwell proceeded to enforce upon the country a rigorous subjection. For nine years he maintained an army of 10,000 men distributed at strategic points, with the function not only of keeping the peace but of exacting what, for so impoverished a country, were enormous taxes. Economically, the condition of the country verged on the desperate. Famine itself threatened, and was averted only by timely relief, sent in by 'the English nation'. The currency problem was acute; lack of money was universal. A diarist of the time speaks of the country as 'layd down in the dust, under the fute of ane enymie, and havie burdings, great skairchtie, dearth and penurie being within the land'.[1]

At the same time, throughout this period, Scotland enjoyed an unwonted peace. The laws were never better kept. Everyone got justice. The endemic strife to which the country was accustomed was brought to an end. There was perfect protection for the traveller

[1] *Nicoll's Diary*, 1650–67.

from molestation. There was freedom of worship, and the people were given peaceable conditions in which to pursue their lawful avocations.

Sectarian disturbance, of course, was rife. The fortunes of the Church were so deeply implicated in the total situation that the pulpit became a chief forum of controversy. Polemical preaching became the rule. 'The prayers and sermons "to the times" were often lively examples of party journalism.' When the Cromwellian Independents, zealous and outspoken in propagating their doctrines and practices, opposed the preachers publicly, calling in question the soundness of their teaching, as we are told they did, for instance, in the New Kirk and Greyfriars in Edinburgh, and when the ministers retaliated, reverence was put to flight and acrimonious disputation banished worship.

A not surprising consequence of these unsettlements during the six years ending in July 1655 was, as the diarist records, that 'the holy and blessed Communion of the blessed Body of our Lord and Saviour Jesus Christ was not celebrated within the town of Edinburgh, neither yet within many other parts of the country, by reason of the troubles and sad condition of the land'.

There were quarters where even the Church's praise was silenced. In 1645, within the Synod of Lothian, the reading of the Scriptures and the singing of Psalms were 'discharged' from the people's worship, and in place of them came in 'lectures by ministers, which continued till the incoming of the English army'. This meant that the people were deprived of one of the rights which it was the aim of the Reformation to secure to them—that of making their voices heard in the worship of God.

Not till after the lapse of eight years—in October 1653—was the right to resume 'the wonted custom of singing of psalms' restored. Apparently even then only limited advantage was taken of this permission, for in 1658 the Synod of Lothian appointed a Committee 'to consider whether or not, in every congregation, when the people are gathered, there should be singing of psalms and reading of chapters both before and after noon on the Sabbath Day'. Three years later, in 1661, the reading of the Scriptures was brought in again, and the Psalms were ordered to be sung, with the addition of the Doxology. This latter injunction appears to have been welcomed, for the worshippers are said to have sung 'with greater devotion than ever before, for all the people rose at the singing of "Glory to the Father, the Son, and the Holy Ghost"'. The sympathies of the diarist are indicated by his record of the fact that singing was 'discharged' under Presbytery, and that the restoration of it took place 'by authority of the bishops'.

The truth is, that music generally in Scotland had fallen on evil days. One heavy blow had befallen it when, after the union of the Crowns, the Court left Edinburgh for London. The removal, with them, of the musicians with whom the Stuarts loved to surround themselves, deprived Scotland of a cultural influence which had enriched at least their own entourage and in some degree affected the life of the people. James I, James III, and James IV in particular did much to

promote music: of the last named it has been said that
his reign 'held nearly all the sunshine of the Renaissance that ever beamed on Scotland'.[1]

But a more widely felt loss befell with the decline
of the pre-Reformation song-schools, and the passing
away of those who had been trained in them. Only
fifteen years after the issue of the 1564 Psalter—in
1579—it was found necessary to pass an Act providing
for the reviving of these schools.

'For instruction of the youth in the art of musik and singing,
quhilk is almaist decayit, and sall schortly decay, without
tymous remeid be providit, oure Soverane Lord, with avise of his
thrie estatis of this present parliament, requeistis the provost,
baillies, counsales and communitie of the maist speciall burrowis
of this realme, and of the patronis and provestis of the collegis,
quhair sang sculis are foundat, to erect and sett up ane sang
scuill with ane maister sufficient and able for instructioun of the
youth in the said science of musik, as they will answer to his
hienes upoun the perrell of their foundationis, and in performing
of his hieness requeist do unto his Majestie acceptable and gude
plesure.'

This Act had some good effect. Aberdeen, Ayr,
Cupar, Dunbar, Dundee, Elgin, Lanark, and St.
Andrews did what was asked, in some cases before the
Act. But no endeavour to galvanize into activity the
failing energies of the schools could succeed. Galvanize
is the right word to use, not vitalize; for what the Act
produced was only an artificial energy, not the vigour of
real life. The specific function for which the schools were
brought into being ceased almost completely when

[1] Andrew Lang: *History of Scotland.*

plain-song and the elaborate polyphonic compositions
which were previously in use were no longer required;
and the psalm-tunes which took their place fell far short
of providing adequate means of keeping the schools
alive. Thus the revival the Act of 1579 induced could
not last. No more than nine years elapsed when the
Town Council of Glasgow showed that they had already
ceased to feel that the obligation laid on them by the
Act required to be respected, for they appropriated
that part of the Common Good which had been devoted to the upkeep of 'the Scuile sumtyme callit the
Sang Scuile', to defray the expenses incurred in connexion with a heavy visitation of the plague. The
decline must already have been again in rapid progress,
when such a flagrant alienation of public money from
its traditional purpose could, even under the stress of
such circumstances, take place without a protest.

The progress of the decline was greatly accelerated
by the invasion of Scotland, from south of the Border,
by a pestilent type of Puritanism, inconceivably arro-
gant and intolerant, which, in the name of a supposedly
superior piety, sought to cast discredit on every form
of art used in association with worship. It was inevitable that music should suffer, as it did desperately,
from the blight which this heresy (Brownism) cast over
the whole of Scottish religion.

The seventeenth century was but begun when it
became evident that a generation was arising which
could not learn the old Psalter tunes. The simple
Common Tunes were written for this new generation.
The musical fashion was changing. The old ecclesias-

tical modes which had long reigned unchallenged were falling into desuetude, and the harmonic system with which we are now familiar was taking its place. Even the great musical artistry displayed in the 1635 Psalter did not avail to save the old tunes. The tide was ebbing fast from the whole system they represented, and it was too late to change it.

In all these circumstances it cannot be wondered at that there was no issue of tunes with the Psalter of 1650, nor any protest against the omission. In point of fact very few tunes were known or sung by the people at that time. When the first collection of tunes for use with the new Psalter was published by an Aberdeen printer in 1666, it contained only twelve tunes. These were: COMMON TUNE, KING'S TUNE, DUKE'S TUNE, ENGLISH TUNE, FRENCH, LONDON (LONDON NEW), STILT (YORK), DUNFERMLINE, DUNDEE, ABBEY, MARTYRS, ELGIN, and, added for local reasons, BON ACCORD (in reports). By the end of the century these twelve were canonized as embodying the accepted and inexpansible musical tradition of the Church of Scotland. At that point the canon was closed, and it remained fixed for a long time subsequently. All twelve (BON ACCORD being an extra) were common-metre tunes. Even the finest of the old tunes in other metres were forgotten. Dr. Beattie confessed his desire that all the psalms not in common metre should be abandoned. Some of the old tunes for these may have lingered on in people's memories. It is difficult otherwise to guess what the tune was to which Margaret Wilson, tied to a stake within the floodmark in the Water of Bladnoch, at Wigtown—there to be drowned when the Solway tide flowed full unless she recanted—sang Psalm 25 from the seventh verse:

> My sins and faults of youth
> do thou, O Lord, forget:
> After thy mercy think on me,
> and for thy goodness great.

For the words are in short metre, and there was no short-metre tune then available except, probably, the one she remembered as sung in the old Psalter to the same Psalm.

In view of these facts the conclusion is irresistible that the true Covenanters' tunes are to be found only within the restricted number named. The probability is that only a few even of these were actually much sung. It is impossible to listen to them without realizing that certain other tunes, which, in our own time, have gathered round them something of the glamour properly belonging to those which the Covenanters may reasonably be supposed to have sung, could never have been used by people whose conceptions of what was fitting for the worship of God are revealed in these grave, dignified, and for the most part plaintive melodies.

In such circumstances congregational singing can have been, at the best, far from exhilarating. So narrow a range of tunes must have deprived it completely of musical interest. Probably it is here that we find the explanation of the well-nigh total absence of allusions to this aspect of public worship from the records of the period; it had become so destitute of variety and therefore so trite and dull, that it made no impression on anyone's mind that seemed to be worth recording. The life had gone out of it.

To what extent singing was practised in the worship of the conventicles it is impossible to say. So far as the historical documents go, it would appear that not much attention was paid to it. Dr. Smellie in his *Men of the Covenant*, writing of those who gathered at the conventicle at East Nisbet in Roxburghshire, picturesquely describes 'their melody swelling in full unison along the hill'. Any such full-throated singing is in the last degree unlikely. Considerations of safety must have been decisive against such a reckless proclamation to the enemy of what was going on. The real situation is indicated by what we are told of Renwick's first public meeting, that it was 'in the remotest recess they could find, most convenient for safety and secrecy, for fear of the enemies'. In the silence of moors, mosses, and hills sound carries far, and singing in such conditions must have meant serious danger or betrayal. Simpson, in his *Traditions of the Covenanters*, gives one incident that supports this. At a conventicle at Darngavel, in Cambusnethan, while the people were 'raising aloft the voice of praise, the melody wafted by the breeze was heard at Blackhall at the moment a trooper happened to call in passing'. The farmer there was friendly to the Covenanters, and anxious to avert danger from them. He set the trooper's suspicions at rest by saying to him, 'Whenever my neighbour at Darngavel shears ane o' his sheep or taks aff ony twa o' his lambs, he sets the hale flock a-bleating.' If the

I

sound heard bore, as it seems to have done, such close resemblance to the cries of sheep in distress, as to persuade a suspicious man that it was that and nothing else, not much could be said of its musical quality. But indeed what else could be expected at a time when even in the most favourable conditions no canons of quality evoked the most casual respect? As a general rule, it may be taken for granted that the perilous circumstances in which conventicles were held made it imperative to omit singing from their worship.

None the less, the publication of the new Psalter in 1650 was unquestionably a great public boon. Apart from other difficulties that made a new version desirable, the number of metres employed in the earlier one made the use of many of the Psalms impossible when musical knowledge declined. The people needed simplicity in the verse as well as in the music, and while to us the excessive use of Common Metre in the new version seems a thing to regret, not least because it banished from use the most splendid of the Reformation melodies, there can be no doubt that one of its chief attractions to those for whose use it was first intended was its large use of the ballad-metre familiar in their traditional songs. The Psalms in that simple metre were easy to memorize, and it became possible to draw upon a wider range of portions because the tunes used were few and suitable to the great majority of them. Probably for that reason the new Psalter passed straight into the affections of the common people. It was a godsend, coming just then, when the Killing Times were not far distant; for when the sufferings of those bitter times arrived, it had won its place in the people's hearts, and its lines were so deeply imprinted upon their memories that it is always the language thus given them for the expression of their emotions, which in the great hours we find upon their lips.

You can imagine what it would be to them. Books in those days were few. The Bible came first. The Psalm-book stood next in honour. It was their constant companion, their book of private devotion, as well as their manual of Church worship. In godly households it was the custom to sing through it in family worship. Thus, in the story of John Goodall we are told that in certain lines of a psalm, used as 'his ordinary in his family worship', he discerned what he took to be the finger of God pointing to the impending fate of his enemies. 'His ordinary' means the portion which fell to be sung on that particular day, as he pursued his custom of singing straight through the Psalter in the devotions of his household. The new version was only eighteen years old when the Killing Times began, yet nowhere in those times—unless perhaps, on the occasion alluded to, on the lips of Margaret Wilson—do you hear any echo of the old one; invariably it is from the new that those who resorted to the Psalms to sustain their souls in hours of anxiety and peril, drew the language of strength and consolation: it was there that they found a voice for the faith, the patience, the courage, and the hope that bore them through those dark and cruel years. That is one reason why these Psalms gather round them sentiments which will always endear them to Scottish folk who know anything of the history of their race. They are steeped in that history. They are stained with the blood of the martyrs, who counted not their lives dear to them that by suffering and sacrifice they might keep faith with conscience and save their country's liberties from defeat.

Chapter 11

The Eclipse begins to pass

WHEN peaceable conditions were restored in Scotland after the Revolution Settlement in 1689, there began, at first privately, then publicly, a national revival of musical interest and culture. In 1695 there was a Grand Concert in Edinburgh, with an orchestra of thirty performers, nineteen of them 'gentlemen of fashion', the rest 'professors' of music. Choral music began to be cultivated in 1720 with the performance of Handel's *Esther*, the first of a succession of his oratorios to be performed in Scotland. In 1728 a society of seventy members was formed for the purpose of holding a weekly concert, and it was rewarded with such enthusiastic support that in 1762 it was able to build St. Cecilia's Hall—now a dreary wreck, but at that time a model concert-hall—at the foot of Niddrie's Wynd. For three-quarters of a century the best music of the time was rendered there, and famous artists from abroad were brought over to discourse it. The Hall was the resort of all the rank and fashion of the capital, and the chief centre of the musical art in Scotland.

Revival of music among the common people, however, appears to have been slow. Robert Fergusson (1750–74) at that very time lamented:

> Nae lasses now, on simmer days,
> Will lilt at bleachin' o' their claes;

Nae herds on Yarrow's bonnie braes
    Or banks o' Tweed
Delight to chaunt their hamely lays
    Sin' Music's deid. . . .

Now foreign sonnets bear the gree
An' cribbit queer variety
O' sounds fresh sprung frae Italy,
    A bastard breed!
Unlike that saft-tongu'd melody
    Which now lies deid.

But popular song was languishing only, not dead. The people must have cherished their traditional songs in private although the narrow religious opinion of the time discouraged them. For Allan Ramsay's *Scots Songs* (1718, 1719) and *Tea-Table Miscellany* (1724), though published without music, named the tunes in a way which showed that he could depend upon popular knowledge to supply them: everybody knew them. And very soon the publication of the music incited others to issue other collections of Scottish songs, with music, which were widely welcomed.

Smollett refers to the Edinburgh concerts in *Humphrey Clinker*, and in one of his letters, dated Edinburgh, August 1756, says: 'The Scots are all musicians. Every man you meet plays on the flute, the violin, or the violoncello, and there is one nobleman [the Earl of Kellie] whose compositions are universally admired.'

A little later—in 1774 and 1775—Captain Topham in his *Letters from Edinburgh* says: 'The degree of attachment which is shown to music in general in this country exceeds belief. It is not only the principal entertainment, but the constant topic of every conversation; and it is necessary not only to be a lover of it, but to be possessed of a knowledge of the science, to make yourself agreeable to society.'

In Aberdeen, progress was no less noteworthy. That region had not been thrown into commotion like the south and the south-west by the Covenanting struggle, and so we find Richard Franck, 'Philanthropist', in his *Northern Memories, calculated for the Meridian of Scotland*, written in 1658, though not published till 1694, describing the travels of a Cromwellian trooper and Independent in Scotland in 1656 and 1657, saying this of Aberdeen: 'Here you shall have such method in your musick, and such order and decorum of song devotion in the church, as you will admire to hear, though not regulated by a cantor or quirister, but only by an insipid parochial clerk.' This may well be believed, for the Aberdeen Song School was still in active existence. Its efficient master at that time was Thomas Davidson, who was partly responsible for a daring musical venture in 1662—the publication of the first book of secular songs to appear in Scotland since the Reformation. Its formal title was *Cantus: Songs and Fancies*, but it is generally known as *Forbes's Cantus*, or as *The Aberdeen Cantus*. Doubtless it would not have appeared when it did but for the new freedom which the Restoration had brought from some of the too restrictive inhibitions the Reformers had imposed.

The publisher, an enterprising printer named John Forbes, while in no way abating his claim to a share in whatever credit might be going, and avowing himself 'ready and most willing in his Generation, to improve his talents and parts', disclaims responsibility for anything but the technical part of the enterprise. In a high-flown Dedication to the Lord Provost, Baillies, and Town Council, he describes them as constituting 'a harmoniously heavenly consort of as many musicians as magistrates', and claims for the city that its musical fame has 'almost overspread Europe'. Here of course imagination and flattery far outsoar the fact; but enough truth underlies the exaggeration to warrant a high measure of honour being accorded to Aberdeen and its rulers for their efforts to keep the flag of music flying in an unusually degenerate age.

The contents of the *Cantus* are not in themselves remarkable. The music is all borrowed from English and Italian sources, and is of a kind with which England had long been familiar, and the words, though Scottish, are not contemporary, the native muse, after such long-continued discouragement and repression, having not yet recovered its voice. They are adapted from poets of the sixteenth century. The significance of the book is in the fact that here was a real attempt to break through the embargo laid for so long upon all music that was not in the narrowest sense religious, and to claim liberation for the spirit of the people from an unnatural and grievously unwholesome restraint.

How narrow the restrictions were within which that spirit was confined was shown by what happened when Forbes, in his admirable zeal, set himself to add to his service to secular music another, much needed, to the

tion [that is to say, without the 'lining' then still in common use].

There is no evidence that these ideas received any practical attention. But decisive changes were now not far away.

Chapter 12

Obstacles to Reform:
I. The Early Precentors

WITH the passing away of the generation that had had the benefit of musical instruction in the pre-Reformation song-schools, the knowledge of music rapidly declined. The schools themselves, except in Aberdeen, began early to fall into disuse.

Extravagant claims have been made for what the pre-Reformation Church did for popular education. The existence of its choir-schools has been taken to imply that the word 'schools', so used, has the same connotation as it has to-day. But it has not. Professor Sanford Terry's statement that Scotland's 'backward civilization was not incompatible with a tradition of education which Knox continued rather than created' does not accord with the facts. Nor do the optimistic representations of the situation made by Professor Edgar in his *Early Scottish Education* correspond to the realities. In point of fact choir-schools were, at the best, not numerous in Scotland. G. G. Coulton says that his researches into the history of the Scottish abbeys, the supposed homes of learning, failed to discover in any of them any traces of such schools. Where they did exist, in the thirteen cathedrals and the thirty-eight collegiate churches existing at the Reformation, the boys in them were few in number. In the thirteenth century Aberdeen provided for no more than 'four singing boys'; later the number was increased to eleven. Glasgow had only six boys. St. Giles's, Edinburgh (then a collegiate church), and Biggar each had four. Bishop Dowden says that in some instances no more than two boys were maintained on the foundation.

Their education was strictly *ad hoc*. 'Music, meaners and virtew' was an Aberdeen description of the results it aimed at producing. The instruction was mainly in reading Latin, though not necessarily in understanding it, and in singing the plain-chant, and latterly the prick-song (written music) required for the services. Probably, too, many of the choristers were like the one in Chaucer's *Prioresses Tale* who, challenged by the child who heard him sing *Alma redemptoris* 'T' expounen him this song in his langage', had to reply, 'I lerne song, I can but smal grammere.' But in any case it is obvious that the educative influence upon the community of such small numbers who had received any choir training must have been very restricted.

In 1643 Parliament enacted that heritors should 'stent' themselves to provide a school in every parish, but the Act soon passed into abeyance. The burgh schools did their best, but the Town Councils could not go beyond what the people allowed them to attempt. The general poverty, the appropriation of the revenues of the Church by the Crown and nobles, made the literal starvation of education inevitable. Teachers were, at the best, paid microscopic and uncertain wages. Exceptions there were, where landowners showed some conscience for their duty: but large expanses of the country had no teacher at all, and were destitute of any kind of educational provision. James Wodrow, father of the historian, told his son that in the days of the Covenant, 'in the heyday of religious fervour', the generality of the people could not read. Proof that he did not exaggerate is evident in the fact that large numbers of those who 'signed' the national Covenant could do no more than adhibit, not their signatures, but only their marks. The truth is, as Professor Mackinnon put it, that 'The Reformed Church drew up a magnificent system of primary, secondary and university education, but the scheme was unfortunately still-born.' The abundant facts which Grey Graham adduces in proof amply justify his assertion that the Reformers' educational system 'remained somewhat of an ideal like the Mosaic legislation in the wilderness —a scheme of perfection to be thwarted by the deep poverty of the country, by the turbulence of parties, by the civil and religious warfare of generations'.[1]

Here we have the basic reason why congregational taste in singing remained static, and so entirely unaffected in its rigid narrowness by the general musical advance throughout the country, that church singing must have been, for people who knew what good music was, nothing less than a torture. Guidance was non-existent. As Livingston says: 'Confessions of Faith, Catechisms and other guides, were formed for the assistance of ministers, teachers, etc., but the poor precen-

[1] Henry Grey Graham, *The Social Life of Scotland in the Eighteenth Century* (London: A. & C. Black, 1899), vol. ii, p. 151.

tors were left to grope in the dark and discover the principles of their art as best they might. Not a page seems to have been furnished for their instruction for one hundred and fifty years.' The old psalm-books containing the tunes of 1564 became scarce. Reprinting was out of the question. The fashion in musical practice had changed: the old modes were becoming obsolete, and apart from the Common Tunes the old books were no longer of any use. In many parts of the country no tune-books of any kind existed; and, had any been available, the state of education would have made the reading of them far from easy.

'Up-taker of the psalm' was the official style given to the leader of the singing. 'Raiser of the psalm' was also used, and 'he that takes up the line'. The name Precentor was not yet commonly in use. Not infrequently the office was combined with that of the Reader, an official who for eighty years after the Reformation had the duty of reading the Scriptures to the people assembled for the Sunday service for the hour before the minister appeared. The Reader's desk continued to be known as the lectern—otherwise 'lateran' or 'lattron'—long after it had ceased to serve for reading, and was used for the leading of the singing. The schoolmaster often held this office. Where there was a Sang Schule the master of it was *ex officio* the precentor. In Haddington, for example, in 1563, the master of the song-school was required to 'uptake the psalms in the Kirk', and in Ayr the occupant of the same office undertook 'to sing in the Kirk the four parts of music, beginning each Sunday at the second bell'.

K

As time went on, it was often difficult to find anyone with even the minimum of the requirements for the office. The remuneration was small. In 1581 the 'fie of the maister of the song scole' at Cupar was £6. 13s. 4d. In 1640 Gilbert Ross acknowledged receipt of 40 merks (Scots)—about £2 sterling—'for his service in reading, singing, and teaching of the school within the city and Machar Kirk' (Aberdeen). And in the Statistical Account of Heriot (1759) it is said of the schoolmaster of the parish, 'He is also precentor, session-clerk, beadle, and grave-digger, and yet his whole income does not exceed £8 per annum.'

Sometimes the dearth of local talent was such that 'wayfaring men' had to be called on to do duty. James Melville, for instance, records in his Diary that in 1570 the laird of Dun in Angus, entertaining a blind man out of charity, found him possessed of a 'singular good voice' and had him appointed 'Doctor' of the Sang Schule, to teach 'the whole psalms in metre, with the tones [tunes] thereof, and sing them in the Kirk'.

Later, the only equipment required was some ability to read, and a voice full and resonant enough to make itself heard over the efforts of the congregation to find and follow the tune. Sometimes the leader was barely literate, and was capable of perpetrating grotesque errors of pronunciation. The number of tunes he knew depended much upon his ability to remember and reproduce what he had heard others sing. It was no uncommon thing for him to know only three or four tunes. At one church a visiting minister was told by the precentor before the service, 'I can sing only twa

tunes, sir, so ye maunna gi'e oot three psalms.' This
might be no loss, for the prescribed number of psalms
to be sung was usually only two.

At Coull in Aberdeenshire the precentor one day
sang all the psalms to a single tune, BANGOR. One of
the congregation remarked to him afterwards, 'Ye
were great on "Bangor" the day, Sandy.' To which the
offended precentor snappishly replied, 'Be't "Bangor",
or be't Dangor, ye got a weel sustained tune, an' hae
nae reason to compleen.'[1]

Occasionally the precentor came to grief in the tune.
Twice, in widely-separated parts of the country, the
present writer has heard the leader start too high, and,
finding that neither he nor his choir could proceed,
stop and say, 'Na, that'll no dae; let's try again', then
launch away on a lower key and come through triumphantly.

Dr. Guthrie recorded the fact that once, when he
was conducting an important service in Free St.
George's, Edinburgh, the precentor broke down so
completely that to end the universal embarrassment,
he rose, and, saying 'Let us pray', brought the incident
to an end.

There were times when rivalries between aspirants
to the office gave rise to actual fracas. There can have
been few such contests as that of which Kelso Abbey,
then used as the parish church, was the scene in 1694,
while the passions aroused by the Revolution Settlement were still running high. Presbyterians and

[1] Nicholas Dickson, *The Kirk and its Worthies* (T. N. Foulis, London and
Edinburgh, 1914), p. 134.

Episcopalians met together in the Abbey, ostensibly for worship. Each party had its own precentor, and feeling between them was so acute that worship was impossible. The Presbyterians had as leader a tuneful weaver from Yetholm, and the Episcopalians were led by the parish schoolmaster, a Master of Arts and a contentious person, Kirkwood by name, who insisted that in virtue of his office he had a prescriptive right to occupy the lectern. When a psalm was given out, the rivals vied with each other in attempting to get first 'off the mark'. The favourite tune of the one was STILT (YORK): that of his rival was LONDON. Both started off together, 'making indeed a sweet Melody, each of them with the help of their Consorts crying and sqweeking aloud, to drown the voices of their opposites'. Peace was restored only when the minister gave the Master of Arts, in the lectern beneath him, 'a rapp on the pate, and snatched the Book out of his hand'. Meantime those in the church who were neutral 'did laugh very heartily'; a great number ran out of doors 'as if a great fire had been amongst them'; and 'some English officers . . . cried out with a loud voice "The People are all gone mad, and the Devil's in the minister".' The dispute did not end until on 22 October 1696 the Synod of Merse and Teviotdale put a stop to the processes with which the Episcopalian claimant had for two years waged a wordy warfare with the Church Courts, by depriving him of all his offices.[1]

Another example of the use of physical violence

[1] Kirkwood's *Plea before the Kirk*, p. 136. Cf. J. F. Leishman's *Linton Leaves*, p. 70.

occurred in Bridge of Teith Church in the days when
the tyranny of the Twelve Tunes still persisted. New
tunes were beginning to be allowed elsewhere, and one
day the precentor, without authorization or warning,
broke into the novel strains of BANGOR when the
psalm was given out. The minister, Mr. Fletcher, sat
for a moment or two dumbfounded, unable to believe
his ears, then rose, seized the pulpit Bible and brought
it down with stupefying force on the head of the
offender beneath him, and dared him ever to be guilty
of such an outrage again.

A curious incident is recorded in the Old Statistical
Account of Caithness.[1] In the days of the last Episcopal
minister of Halkirk, there was no singer of the psalms
in the church, apart from the letter-gae or precentor,
but a gardener at Braal. This man sang so loud, and
with such a large open mouth, that a mischievous
young fellow was tempted to throw a stone into the
gaping cavity. He succeeded, broke the singer's teeth,
and brought the singing, and the service, to an end.
The marksman took to his heels, but was pursued by
his victim's sons, and the upshot was a desperate fight.

Scenes of such unseemliness were far from typical.
As a rule the precentor was a person of some consequence in the community. On Sunday he occupied a
position only a little lower than that of the minister—
either at the lectern or in the lower compartment of a
two-decker pulpit. Quite commonly he wore a black
stuff gown, and sometimes even bands. In later days
also he performed what to children was always a

---

[1] *Old Statistical Account,* xix. 49.

fascinating variation upon the somewhat dreary proceedings: from some hidden receptacle he produced a
long piece of cardboard bearing in large letters the
name of the tune to which the announced Psalm was to
be sung, and, fitting a peg underneath it into a socket
in the ledge of his desk, turned the card to this side
and to that so that everyone might see it and know,
without further intimation, what the tune was to be.

These circumstances, and the eminence he occupied,
were apt to induce him to assume airs which his qualifications did not justify.

Allan Ramsay, in his *Christ's Kirk on the Green*—a
continuation of James I's poem bearing that title, only
one canto of which was written by the royal author—
drew the following picture of a precentor in unofficial
and social mood:

> The letter-gae of haly rhime
>   Sat up at the boord-head,
> And a' he said 'twas thought a crime
>   To contradict indeed:
> For in clerk lear he was right prime,
>   And could baith write and read,
> And drank sae firm till ne'er a styme
>   He could keek on a bead
>   or book that day.

Historically Allan was wrong. The letter-gae, reader,
or precentor, was no pre-Reformation personage: his
day came after the Reformation. But the picture
delineates the type of man who often filled the office
in days near Allan's own time.

Of a still later type Dr. Beattie of Aberdeen, in 1829,
had a complaint to make.

'I wish', he wrote, 'they [the precentors] were obliged to put on a serious air while they are employed [in their duty]. Many of them do so, and have a right sense of those decorums that belong to an act of worship. But some affect the appearance of total inattention; and, while they sing, cast their eyes to every corner of the church, and turn their head at every opening of the door, as if they had to satisfy their audience that they could keep the tune, without once thinking of what they were about.'

For a long time there were no choirs to compete with them for attention. It is true that in 1587 the Kirk Session of Glasgow ordered that 'Mr. William Struthers, teacher of music, shall sing in the High Kirk ... and appoint four men to sit beside him', and in the following year ordered 'that the sangsters in toun sing with Mr. Struthers on Sunday'. Stirling Kirk Session in 1621 decided 'that the pulpet and Reederis letrun sal be taine doune and reedefeit again' and that the tradesmen in the process of reconstruction should 'mak commodious seattis about the fit thairof for the maister of the sang schuil and his bairnis to sit on, for singing the psalmes in the tyme of the holie serveice of the Kirk'. But these cases were exceptional, and in the common experience of the churches the precentor reigned alone over the people's offering of praise.

Chapter 13

Obstacles to Reform: II. The People

WHEN the leadership of the Church's praise was in such untrained and incompetent hands, the singing of the congregation could not be of any higher quality. They also were for the most part without knowledge of any better practice than their precentors exhibited, and strange things were to happen before improvement could take place. Indeed the sense of the ludicrous must be kept firmly in restraint, if we are to be able to imagine how the facts about to be described could be consistent with reverence, much less with the worship of which for many people they were undoubtedly the medium.

In one practice, for example, which ultimately became general, the precentor led the way, and the people were not slow to do likewise: the practice of adorning the tune with 'graces'. You may hear it in the Highlands to this day. There have been many speculations as to the origin of the Highland way of singing psalms. One suggestion is that it is a survival of the Celtic Church mode of singing. Unfortunately, no living soul can tell what the Celtic Church singing was like; nor will anyone ever be able to tell until, as a witty Irish scholar put it, 'radio becomes retroactive', for no written trace of it exists. Another impossible idea is that it was brought from Sweden by the Highland soldiers who returned from serving, as many did, in the

army of Gustavus Adolphus. But Gustavus was a
Lutheran, and the Scottish soldiers serving under him
could have learned no sacred music in his service but
the German chorales; he and his troops sang one of the
greatest of these, before action, on the morning of the
day on which he fell at Lützen. Once more, it is suggested that the graces characteristic of pipe-music
may have given rise to the practice. These may have
encouraged it, and perhaps have made even extrava-
gance in it seem not unnatural. But its real source must
be sought elsewhere.

The use of 'graces' was an ancient one: it had its
origin in the ninth century. It began with the development of the tropes, which consisted of decorations
imposed upon the simple plain-chant; passages were
inserted in the tune in which 'one syllable flowered out
into a passage of several notes'; then the extra notes
were used to accommodate extra words of a character
consonant with the original theme. This practice was
carried to great lengths in the Middle Ages. It is easy
to understand how tempting it was to skilled choristers
to embellish the simple tune with such decorations.
Bishop W. H. Frere, a distinguished expert in medieval
Church music, commenting on the skill exhibited by
composers and singers in inserting elaborate passages
at intervals in the *conducti* and *organa* of the thirteenth
century reproduced in *A St. Andrews Music Manuscript*,
edited by Prof. J. H. Baxter, remarks: 'It is the old
story of the tropes again, and of the glorifications
inserted into the harmonized plainchant; for the singer
will have his roulade, his vocalise, and his jubilus.' An

entrancingly delightful exercise it must have been for the singers, but it was a potent factor in the debasement of plainsong.

In the eighteenth century Italian opera made the practice popular. Musicians of the first rank made large use of it. Handel has made us familiar with it by importing it from his operatic music into his oratorios. Bach's most famous son devoted no fewer than eight chapters of one of his works to a full discussion of the subject.

'Nobody', he declared, 'doubts the necessity of ornaments. They are quite indispensable. They connect the notes and give life to them. Where necessary they add to them a particular expression and weight. They render the meaning clearer; be it sad or merry or otherwise they contribute something towards it. An indifferent composition is made tolerable by them, and the best melody, without them, is empty and lacking in significance. ... Those performers who possess sufficient ability may insert ornaments beyond those I prescribe, but they must be careful to do this in the proper places and without doing violence to the general expression of the composition.'[1]

Unfortunately performers who did *not* 'possess sufficient ability' were apt to arrogate to themselves the right to use this liberty at will. In the worst days of psalmody in Scotland, untutored precentors could not resist the temptation to invent their own ornamentations, and the people followed suit, garnishing the tunes with unauthorized shakes and quavers very much as their spirits moved them.

---

[1] Carl Phillip Emanuel Bach, *Versuch über die wahre Art des Klavier zu spielen*, 1753; tr. *The Oxford Companion to Music*, article on 'Ornaments', p. 674.

When the choir movement began in the mid-eighteenth century, the reduction and extinction of this abuse was one of its necessary aims. Some precentors, however, who were expected to be agents of reform, gave their countenance to them. Thus Cornforth Gilson, whom Edinburgh Town Council brought from Durham to lead the reform movement and to organize choirs in the city, said in the preface to a small collection of tunes he issued for the use of those he taught: 'Some tunes are wrote entirely plain, without any grace, and when sung will appear very insipid for want of *appoggiature* (a small hanging-note), unless it be sung by a Master, who will naturally place the *appoggiature* and adject the graces according to his own Taste.'

Much sounder was the counsel of a native-born teacher and publisher of music, Robert Bremner. In the preface to his *Rudiments of Music* (1756) he has much to say about the evils of grace-notes. He advises precentors to have nothing to do with them, as they will lead to nothing but confusion, and says some things which shed much light on the consequences of the practice:

'Had these nonsensical graces been the same everywhere, it would have been the less matter, but every congregation, nay, every individual, had different graces to the same note, which were dragged by many to such immoderate length that one corner of the church, or the people in one seat, had sung out the line before another had half done: and from the whole there arose such a mass of confusion and discord as quite defaced this noblest part of Divine worship.

'Endeavouring once [he continues] to convince an old man

who was precentor in a country church how absurd he rendered the music by allotting so many different sounds to one syllable, when there was only one intended, he replied with a good deal of briskness that he believed that the people of the present generation knew nothing of the matter: for his master was allowed to understand that affair thoroughly, and he told him that there ought to be eight quavers in the first note of Elgin tune.

'I know the argument you use is that in giving out the tune you are allowed to sing some time alone, till the congregation know what tune you are singing, and therefore you grace these few notes to make them more agreeable to yourself and the audience, but that after they join, you grace no more. This is a very groundless reason; for would you only take the trouble to name the tune you are to sing before you begin, the congregation would strike in at the first note.'

No great exercise of imagination is needed to realize the impression produced on those not familiar with it by a kind of singing in which the tune was hardly identifiable amid the graces that smothered it. It is said that one Italian musician—probably one of those who came, late in the eighteenth century, to perform at the concerts in St. Cecilia's Hall, Edinburgh—finding himself free on a Sunday forenoon, wandered up the High Street. As he passed the Tron Church the service there was nearing its end. The doors being thrown open by the beadle during the closing act of praise, the Italian paused and listened in amazement to the discordant sounds that came pouring out upon his ears. 'What on earth are these horrible sounds I hear?' he asked the beadle. 'That', came the answer, 'is the people praising God.' 'And do the people really believe their God likes to hear that dreadful noise?' 'To be sure,' the beadle answered; 'of course He does.' 'Then all I can say', was the foreigner's rejoinder, 'is, that their God can have no ear for music', and in shocked silence he walked away.

If this condition of things existed in the capital city of the country, it may be assumed that it was worse elsewhere. So late as the beginning of the nineteenth century Mrs. Smith of Baltiboys (a Grant of Rothiemurchus) in her delightful *Memoirs of a Highland Lady*, describes a service of that time in the now discarded Rothiemurchus old Parish Church. The minister gave out the Psalm, read as many verses as were to be sung, in a drawling sing-song. Then

'he stooped over the pulpit to hand his little book to the precentor, who then rose and calling aloud the tune—"St. George's Tune", "Auld Aberdeen", "Hundred and Fifteen", &c.—began himself a recitative of the first line on the keynote, [and the tune was] taken up and repeated by the congregation; line by line he continued in the same fashion, thus doubling the length of the *exercise*, for really to some it was no play—serious severe screaming quite beyond the natural pitch of the voice, a wandering search after the air by many who never caught it, a flourish of difficult execution and plenty of the *tremolo* lately come into fashion. The dogs seized this occasion to bark (for they always came to the Kirk with the family), and the babies to cry. When the minister could bear the din no longer he popped up again, again leaned over, touched the precentor's head, and instantly all sound ceased. The long prayer began . . .'[1]

In the summer of 1855 Sir John Millais and his household attended the Free Church service in Glenfinlas. Millais's brother William wrote afterwards:

[1] *Memoirs of a Highland Lady*, edited by Lady Strachey (London, John Murray, 1898), p. 205.

'The service to us was somewhat comical, and we could hardly stay it out. The precentor was a little very bow-legged man, with the wheeziest of voices, and sang the first line of the paraphrase [i.e. psalm] alone, whilst his little shaggy terrier, the image of his master, joined in the piteous howl. The other lines were sung by the congregation, assisted by a few collies. I afterwards tackled the little precentor, and asked him why he didn't have an organ. "Ah, man, would you have us take to the devil's band?" he replied.'[1]

This type of singing appears to have been general in Scotland in the degenerate period. Stevenson in no wise exaggerated when, in *Weir of Hermiston*, he said that 'the nasal psalmody, full of turns and trills and graceless graces, seemed the essential voice of the Kirk itself upraised in thanksgiving'. And Scott had good reason for making Vich Ian Vohr, in *Waverley*, say of his Presbyterian hostess in Edinburgh, 'O Baron! if you heard her fine counter-tenor admonishing Kate and Matty in the morning, you, who understand music, would tremble at the idea of hearing her shriek in the psalmody of Haddo's Hole' (one of the churches into which St. Giles's was then divided).

It is difficult to conceive of singing of such a sort awakening nostalgic longings in the breast of a Scot abroad. Yet such a thing did happen. Lady Anne Barnard, daughter of the Earl of Lindsay and authoress of 'Auld Robin Gray', when at the Cape with her husband, who was Colonial Secretary to Lord Macartney, wrote in her diary, about the beginning of the nineteenth century, of walking to the church there.

---

[1] *The Order of Release*, edited by Admiral Sir William James (London, John Murray, 1947), p. 204.

'We listened', she said, 'with reverence to all we understood, and with smiles to the horrid discords with which a Presbyterian congregation assails the ears—a discord to me now more pious in its sounds of willing praise than all the organs or hired choir-singers in the world, and exceeded by nothing in the sensations it awakens but by a congregation of converted Hottentots joining in one hymn.'[1]

From all this it is possible to understand why a Highland minister, in the General Assembly debate on one occasion on the Psalmody Report, declared that when things musical were at their worst, no words in Scripture better described his feelings when the congregation's exercises in praise came to an end, than those which at the beginning of the twentieth chapter of Acts record the quelling of the riot of the Ephesians in defence of their worship of Diana: 'After the uproar was ceased . . .'

When practices like 'gracing' and 'lining' had long had firm hold upon the people, it was far from easy to put an end to them. For the Scots are nothing if not tenacious. Hume Brown did not err when he wrote of 'that "narrow intensity" which is the special note of Scottish genius and character'. Nor was Grey Graham wrong when he said of the Scots of the eighteenth century:

'These people's independence, like the Whiggism of their politics and the Covenanting in their religion, was intensely conservative—conservative of their own rights, of their old faith, customs, practices. . . . In fact, radical as the Scottish temperament is called, it was then not the radicalism of those who uproot old institutions and seek out new paths; it was

[1] *Memoirs*, in *Lives of the Lindsays.*

really a conservatism as keen as that of the Jacobites in resistance to change, whether in dress, in farming and in social customs, or in theology and worship.'

'Resistance to change!' That, throughout the generations, has been a persistent habit in Scottish religious practice. There is truth to our national character as well as humour in the story of the dying beadle who, being asked by his son, who was to succeed him in office, whether he had any parting instruction to give him, replied that he had but one thing to say, and that was, 'Resist a' improvements'.

Here is the explanation of the obstinate refusal to relax the tyranny of the Twelve Tunes by the addition of a single new tune throughout the course of a century, and of the determination to keep outside of the church-door the influences which were creating a musical revival elsewhere throughout the country. The common people had for centuries been excluded by the musicians from any share in the Church's praise; but once they got hold of the easy, straight-forward Common Tunes, they reversed the situation: they assumed the mastery, and would permit the singing of nothing else. They did not know it, but this was their revenge for the wrong done to generations of their forefathers: they closed, locked, and barred the door of the church against any innovation upon the new and narrow musical tradition which their resolute ignorance imposed upon the Church.

'Resistance to change!' Here also is the explanation of not a few of the minor secessions which have chequered Scottish Church history. The least degree

'THE STOOL OF REPENTANCE' BY DAVID ALLAN

Showing a precentor in his desk, below the preacher, in a Scottish kirk of the early eighteenth century

A HIGHLAND CONGREGATION IN THE ACT OF
SINGING, 1855
Sketch by Sir J. E. Millais (*see pp.* 141–2)

of departure from traditional usage was met by determined and sometimes extreme resistance. Thus, for
example, in Kirkcaldy, Johnshaven, Tough in Aberdeenshire, and Langton in Berwickshire, so many
people forsook the parish churches as to form Secession
congregations, by way of protest when the practice of
lining-out the psalms was given up. 'These determined
prejudices', wrote Dr. G. W. Sprott, 'were carried to
the ends of the earth. I remember old Scotsmen in the
colonies who never entered church because the line
was not read out as they had been accustomed to hear
it in the Old Country.'

In other places resistance to this change was not carried quite so far. The abandoned practice was sometimes
continued at home where no veto could be interposed
to suppress it. There were cases in which something
else than affection for a custom for which all justifi-
cation had departed, was the reason for adhering to
it in private practice. Thus 'Jeems the Doorkeeper',
of whom Dr. John Brown wrote affectionately in one of
his most charming papers, maintaining in his solitude
'what he called, with a grave smile, *family* worship,
morning and evening, never failing, . . . not only sang
his psalm, but gave out or chanted *the line* in great style;
and on seeing [the Doctor] one morning surprised at
this, he said, "Ye see, John, *oo*"—meaning himself and
his wife—"oo began that way".'[1]

It was in a very different spirit that Ellen Glendin-
ning, a member of Liddesdale Secession Church,

[1] Dr. John Brown, *Horae subsecivae, Third Series* (Edinburgh, David Douglas,
1889), p. 287.

L

chanted the run-line, as it was called, faithfully in her own solitary home-worship. She hotly resented the decision of the Kirk Session to stop the practice in church, but defiantly took what satisfied her as revenge by ceasing singing in church, noting carefully the passages sung, and then singing them alone, run-line and all, in her private worship at home.[1]

The same kind of obstinate self-will evinced itself in another direction. Individual members became a law to themselves not only in making their own variants upon the tune in which the precentor did his best to lead them, but in singing another tune altogether, much as the musicians of the Middle Ages had done in the worst days of the abuse of polyphony. W. A. Gray of Elgin used to tell of a north-countryman who in the early days of the choir-movement was asked by a neighbour, home-going from church, what he thought of the 'band', as the choir was then called. 'Band?' was the scornful answer; 'I never heed the band; I stick to "Bangor".'

A Berwickshire tale is told of a late-comer entering church and slipping into a back seat while the opening singing was in progress. 'What are they singing?' he whispered to his neighbour, who was singing lustily. 'I no ken', was the answer in an idiom of that countryside; 'I no ken; I'm at the AULD HUNDERT.'

Another incident, in Berwick-on-Tweed, belongs to a later time, but is apposite in this connexion. It happened in the great ministry of the first Principal Cairns in Wallace Green Church. It was in the days

[1] Tait, *Border Church Life*, vol. ii, p. 337.

when repeating-tunes were in favour. An old and
honoured member of the congregation objected vehe-
mently to the tune DEVIZES because it had a 'repeat'
in the last line. His protests were unheeded. In the
course of time a new Psalter was introduced, in which
DEVIZES appeared shorn of its repeat. By that time the
old objector had become so enamoured of the form he
had once abhorred that he protested strongly against
its being abandoned. Again his protests were ignored.
But he did not submit: he persisted in singing the
repeat alone when everyone else had ended. His
idiosyncrasy was tolerated, with what patience was
possible. But on one occasion Dr. William Graham of
Liverpool, assisting Dr. Cairns, was mystified by the
strange quavering, unmusical solo at the end of every
verse. Dr. Cairns explained the situation, and said that
they thought it best just to let the old man have his
way. 'I see,' said Graham, 'you just leave him to his
own—DEVIZES.'

Such *laissez faire*, however, could be destructive of
the spirit of worship. Especially in the days when, in
the absence of tune-books and choirs and leaders with
more than the minimum of skill in leading a congregation, the consequence of so many untutored people
following their own vagrant will, and keeping but the
barest vocal contact with the tune, must have been
disastrous. The phraseology used by a writer in the
Aberdeen Intelligencer in April 1785, when reform was definitely begun, may not have been judiciously chosen,
but it will not be questioned that he had warrant for
his language when he deplored 'the genteeler sort of

the audience being silent in this part of divine service', and expressed the hope that the removal of 'the un-couthness and harshness which no doubt must have been irksome to every one who had an ear for music' would induce 'the gentlemen and ladies' who had taken refuge in silence not to 'think it below them to employ their excellent voices in the praises of that great God who bestowed them, and in inflaming the heart to devotion, and not to leave this heavenly exercise as formerly to the lowest of the people'.

Chapter 14

The Rise of the Choir Movement

IN 1753 the leader needed for effective reform appeared. He was Thomas Channon, an Englishman, and almost certainly a Methodist. At that time he was a private in the 20th Foot Regiment, then lying at Aberdeen and commanded by Lieut.-Colonel Wolfe, afterwards General Wolfe of Heights of Abraham fame. An interest in music manifested itself among the soldiers. Some of them were heard practising church music in another than what was in Aberdeen the customary way. On inquiry it was found that their leader was Channon, and that he not only possessed a remarkable gift for teaching and conducting, but was willing to make his services available to others besides his comrades. His discharge from the army was applied for by certain unnamed members of the Synod of Aberdeen, and was granted by Lieut.-General Bland, commanding officer of the garrison, with a view to Channon devoting himself entirely to the task of instructing church people who were willing to be taught to sing—as it was phrased—'in the reformed way'.

Strangely, however, it was not in Aberdeen itself that his operations began, nor even in Aberdeen Presbytery, but twenty miles away, up Donside, at Monymusk, in the Presbytery of Garioch. It has always been a subject of speculation why the movement which was presently to spread over the whole country started, not in town or city, but in a purely agricultural country-side. There can be little doubt that the explanation is, that the laird of Monymusk estate, which was practically co-extensive with the parish, was mainly responsible for financing the movement in its beginnings and for giving it in its early stages guidance and practical support. Sir Archibald Grant, 2nd Baronet of Monymusk, the moving spirit whose identity in this matter has been so long unrecognized, was in every way an enlightened and progressive man. After ten years in Parliament he devoted his notable gifts to the development of his estate. He was a pioneer in agriculture and afforestation in the north-east. He is reported to have planted an almost incredible number of trees on an estate deplorably neglected when he came to it, and now remarkable for its sylvan beauty. He developed local industries, tried glass-making, began also the polishing of granite, thus anticipating one of the great future industries of Aberdeen. Every means within his power to advance the social and educational betterment of the people living under his care, he was instant and eager to use.[1]

Among other interests which he fostered was that of music. In 1748, before Channon was heard of, he instructed the schoolmaster to select the best voices from among the children and form a small choir in the parish church. 'Take measures', he wrote, 'for the church choir, and get all you can to join properly in praise, and to give books and premiums to encourage hopeful children; to read the line of Psalms plain and not drone

[1] *Monymusk Papers* (Scottish History Society).

the reading or singing: the elders to tell this in their respective quarters. . . . Sing the new psalms allowed by the Assembly, and none but choice psalms at all times.' By 'new psalms' he must have meant the first edition of the Paraphrases, issued experimentally in 1745. He thus acted ahead of the Assembly, for thirty-six years were yet to elapse before the edition we now know was finally adjusted.

He was himself interested practically in music, had an organ installed in his library, and there, when Channon came, the choir practices were held, the organ, it is said, accompanying them—a remarkable fact for those times. In church on Sundays, being himself apparently a singer, he sat beside the choir.

In those days, the use of the words of the Psalms themselves in choir-practice was regarded as a kind of irreverence, and practice-verses[1] were used instead. One such verse, which doubtless belongs to that time, ran thus:

> How lovely is thy dwelling-place,
>   Sir Archie Grant, to me;
> The home-park and the policies,
>   How pleasant, sir, they be.

A good choir was soon under training at Mony-musk, and when their proficiency was sufficiently advanced, Channon took the best of his singers into the adjacent parishes, to demonstrate his methods and propagate what soon became a widespread and enthusiastic movement.

The reforms he initiated were these:[2] I. As to the

---

[1] See Chapter 15.   [2] Scots Magazine, 1755.

melody: (1) choosing the best of the old tunes, com-
posing some new ones, and collecting others from the
best sources; (2) teaching the tune 'truly and plain,
without quavering or any kind of affectation'; (3) getting his singers 'to observe the proper time, without
which all must run to confusion'. II. As to the harmony:
it was pointed out that though introduced at the Reformation, as books of that time show,[1] and continued
in some measure until late, it had through inattention
declined by degrees till it had become so entirely lost
that very few had any idea of

'this great effect in music, which is so proper to give it the
grandeur and solemnity requisite in church. Consequently, the
tenor part (the melody) engrossed attention, and people
imagining they might perform it according to their various
humours, the greatest confusion was soon introduced, and the
melody entirely lost in many places. This shows by experience
that if harmony is once disregarded, melody likewise will soon
come to nothing.'

Not much had been done before murmurs of disapproval began to be heard locally. Objection was particularly made to Channon's use of the pitch-pipe to
ensure precision in the key of what was to be sung:
'a newfangled profanation of the Sabbath', it was said,
'was introduced by singing the psalms at church with
a herd-boy's whistle, which gave great offence to many
serious Christians.'

Favourable reports of what was happening, however,
reached Aberdeen, and aroused such eager interest
that 'certain of the magistrates, ministers, and principal inhabitants' combined to invite Channon to visit

---

[1] This idea, of course, was mistaken.

the city with his singers and give a demonstration of
what he was doing. On 2 January 1755 he responded
to the invitation. He took with him seventy of his best
singers from Kintore and Fintray—'18 basses, 30 tenors
(5 of whom sang counter in the 4-part tunes), and
22 female voices for treble and cantus, as the one or the
other was preferred'.

In the New Church (the present West Church of
St. Nicholas, then recently rebuilt), to a great audience,
they gave convincing evidence of the revolutionary
nature of the 'reformation' that was beginning.[1] A
contemporary record says that the singers 'carried on
the different parts in perfect harmony, and with the
greatest exactness in time, very much to the satisfaction of a numerous audience'.

The satisfaction, however, was by no means general.
The Kirk Session held on 20 January what was virtually
an indignation meeting (a writer of the time says that
they 'hurried their act'), and solemnly passed the
following resolution:

'The Session being fully met and convened, and taking into
consideration the specimen of music that was given in this church
on the 2nd of January instant, after divine service, do unanimously
give it as their opinion that the tunes of the said specimen
should not be introduced into public worship. And they appoint
their precentors to sing *only, in all time coming,* the twelve church
tunes commonly sung in churches of Scotland, and printed in
parts, and recommend to the precentors to sing the same in
proper time. And appoint this act to be read from the pulpits
next Lord's Day, with proper exhortations from the ministers;

[1] A copy of the programme of what was sung will be found in
Chapter 16.

that all may learn their common tunes, and parents may see that their children be taught them.'

A shrewd commentator on this edict pointed out that the Kirk Session, in enjoining that the twelve tunes referred to should be sung, were really themselves guilty of innovating, inasmuch as many of the twelve had never been sung at all; and he stated as a fact that an Aberdeen precentor had, not long before, introduced three tunes into his church—ABBEY, DUNFERMLINE, and NEWTOUN (LONDON NEW)—none of which, so far as was known, had ever been heard there before, and which were therefore actually new, although all of them were in the fixed canon of the twelve.

The Session's resolution represented conservative opinion, of which another characteristic expression was this: 'If the Apostle's advice, "Let all things be done to edifying, and follow the things that make for peace" be good ... the innovation is bad; for that it has occasioned such disturbance, distraction, alienation, division, and heart-burnings, that the 1745 was but a jest to it.'

The Presbytery, appealed to for action in support of the protesters, took refuge in the plea that the matter was not formally before them. The provincial Synod proved more courageous. They resolved in May that, 'considering how much the teaching of church music has been neglected for many years past in this country, and that in consequence the singing of psalms in our public worship has been now of a long time performed in such a manner as evidently shows the necessity of a reformation in most congregations; ... earnestly recommend to people of all ranks within their bounds to embrace every opportunity that offers, of being taught to perform that part of divine service in a regular manner, so as to

sing plainly and in just time. And particularly they recommend
to all ministers within their bounds, magistrates of towns, and
heritors of landward parishes, to exert themselves to use every
prudent and reasonable method in getting their respective
congregations to be taught properly, as occasion shall offer.'

This enlightened and judicious counsel was unfortunately not taken by the more extreme of the objec-
tors. Some of these, in Old Aberdeen, complaining
that they could expect no countenance from the
Church judicatories, took the law into their own hands,
and 'attempted to disconcert the regularity in singing
by noise and discord'. They suborned a small number
of shrill-voiced boys, who were no doubt happy to be
encouraged in such a ploy, to be on the watch when the
minister was giving out the first line of the psalm, and
before he had finished it, 'to take up with an extraordinary exertion of voice, a different tune from what
they knew the precentor and the rest of the congregation were to sing'. Such unruly on-goings, destructive
of all order and reverence in the worship, could of
course not be tolerated. The boys were cited to appear
before the magistrate, who 'inflicted a punishment for
this misbehaviour, suited to the age of the offenders,
and in open court admonished everybody to beware
of such proceedings in the future'.

Among those present when this admonition was
given was a weaver of Old Aberdeen, Gideon Duncan
by name. He had been a member of the choir of St.
Machar's, but, taking offence at something said to him
there about his 'petulant and disrespectful behaviour',
threw himself into violent opposition to the new

movement. Carrying his vindictiveness to an extreme, he sought the most public way of expressing it. He published his intention of making a disturbance. At the Sunday service, instead of sitting as formerly with the singers, he took his seat at a strategic point in 'the body of the Kirk', opposite to the precentor, ready for action. He had a good strong voice, and had never before been known to sing out of time. Now, however, he 'sang the last notes louder and drew them out longer than the precentor, so as to interfere with him when he read out the next line, and confuse the regular singers'. What disorder and hubbub followed may be easily imagined.

The inevitable result was a summons to appear before the magistrate to answer a charge of 'raising a noise and making a tumult' to the disturbance of the people in their worship. The case against Gideon was clear, and he was 'decerned to pay £50 Scots fine and £6 Scots expenses of plea, to find security for his good behaviour for two years, and to be imprisoned till he should obtemper the sentence'.

His answer was an appeal to the Court of Session in Edinburgh. The case was tried on 24 July before a court over which Lord Auchinleck (father of James Boswell) presided.

The Senatus of King's College presented the case against Duncan in a statement which, after detailing the facts, concluded with these observations, which have a much wider application than to the case that evoked them:

'This is a sort of contest whether the old and barbarous custom, proceeding without decency or comeliness in this part of divine worship, shall prevail, or if a regular and uniform order of performing it shall be established. Old custom is the idol of the stupid part of the vulgar: however absurd, unprofitable, or even wrong it may be, they are prone to maintain it as a sacred law; and there are never wanting factious leaders, or false brethren of weak hearts or bad and selfish views, to inflame this ignorant zeal. If these incendiaries are properly checked in their first attempts, not by persecution or violence, which adds fewel to enthusiasm and force to faction, but by the authority of law and exercise of justice, which is ever respectable in the eyes of the people and never fails to command their obedience and submission, the rage of opposition ceases, they blame their bad leaders as seducers from their duty, and soon delight in that reformation which at first they blindly treated as apostasy from the truth.'

Gideon's answer showed that he was either a man of shrewd, if litigious, ability, or—more probably—had abler men to help him in framing his plea and financing his law-process. His arguments are worth quoting.[1]

'Of late', he said, 'certain ladies and gentlemen in Old Aberdeen, and with them the masters of the college, having taken up a conceit that that part of worship [singing] was protracted to too great a length, and that the church tunes were not compositions of a fashionable taste, and were not sung with all the musical art, attempted to introduce a new method of singing, greatly quicker than the former, and to bring in new tunes, consisting of three parts, tenor, treble, and bass, altogether unknown to the congregation, excepting a few who were purposely instructed, the consequence of which was no small confusion, as the audience consisted mostly of farmers and mechanics, who had neither time nor ability to learn this new method, yet could not think

[1] See *Scots Magazine*, 1755.

of being debarred from praising God, a privilege which they had ever enjoyed.

'He had been persuaded to join in "these their concertos" with the thirty or forty people in the college loft (in St. Machar's) who performed their several parts after the new quick method, while the rest of the congregation continued to sing in the slow solemn way to which they had ever been accustomed: and this caused irregularity, the precentor having very often to read out the second line before the congregation were done with singing the first, and if he was not so good-natured as to stop for the congregation, the whole became a scene of confusion.

'Seeing this with great regret, after consultation with others, who were averse to every innovation in religious worship, he resolved to abandon the new method, which he looked upon as in its nature indifferent, but in its consequence sinful. He put his resolution into practice.

'No disturbance happened on the Sunday libelled but what arose from the nature of the thing, from the difference between the two methods of singing, and no more than happened for several Sundays before, excepting only that the precentor gave out the line in a greater hurry that day than he had done formerly; that the disturbance was caused by this hurry, and not by the petitioner or the congregation singing longer than was proper and usual; and in short that the petitioner's crime was, singing in the old manner, and that the whole congregation were art and part in the crime.

'He would not enter into a disquisition concerning the merits of the two methods of singing; though perhaps it might be no heterodox doctrine to maintain that the mind intent upon the particular part of the music to be performed would not be fixed with due attention on the Supreme Being, the great object of its contemplation; that it could not rise to that height of rapture and devotion while it attended to the quavers and semi-quavers, etc.

'He drew serious attention to the consequences attending the refusal of his bill. It must of necessity have the effect to restrain every Christian from joining in the praises of God unless he can bear a part in the new method of singing and can sing the tenor, treble, or bass of the new musical compositions which most part of the congregations in Scotland have neither time nor ability to learn. He must be forgiven to consider the refusal of the bill as a declarator and interdict that no person has a right, nor shall have for the future, under a penalty, to sing psalms, unless he understands music perfectly as to be able to bear a part in complex compositions which few understand and still fewer can execute.'

This specious pleading had no effect; the bill was refused on 9 August, and Gideon, after the blaze of publicity his action had directed upon him, disappeared from the vision of history. Some of those, however, who shared his antipathy to the new singing did not hesitate to express it in other ways than by argument. There is a written record of the fact that on the occasion of one of Channon's visits to the East Kirk, Aberdeen, with a choir from Fintray,

'the good folks did not relish the "indecent and new-fashioned" strains that were exhibited, and their fervour stimulated them to commence a very rude assault on the singers and [the] magistrates who took them under their protection. The Bede House being then in existence, the unfortunate choristers were hastily marched into it, where they remained until they could safely take their departure.'

In spite of all opposition, the movement spread, especially in the country districts. In July one inquirer into the results of it wrote as follows:

'The influence of the music has been so powerful that in eleven country parishes where it has either taken effect or is carrying on, I have not been able, after a very minute enquiry, to hear of six persons who have deserted their churches on that account, and I have been assured that in most of them the congregations are thronged, the collections greater, and the communicants more numerous than formerly.'

The eleven parishes referred to were, in the order of time: Monymusk, Cluny, Kemnay, Midmar, Kintore, Fintray, Rayne, Old Meldrum, Kennethmont, Toway (Towie), and Dalmoak (Drumoak).

Choirs became so large that 'singing lofts' had to be built for them. The loft indeed was a notable feature of the architecture of the period. In 1754 in Kintore 'the new Loft which the Earl of Kintore had built and gave free to those who were taught to sing, contained about 120 people, and had greatly slacken'd the body of the church'. In Huntly the new loft was divided into three parts—one for those who sang the cantus or treble, another for the tenor, and the third for the bassus. Alas that it should have to be recorded that the pioneer parish, Monymusk, should amid all this enthusiasm have fallen from grace. It had to be reprimanded by the Presbytery for misapplying £120 Scots, prior to 1781, to provide a Leader of music, and, a year later, for using the proceeds of a Mortification bequeathed by Lord Cullen, father of Sir Archibald Grant, for education in the parish, 'in paying for a Singing Loft for which no rent [i.e. seat rent] is exacted'.

The quality of the choir-training in Channon's time appears to have been remarkably high, for when John Wesley paid the first of two visits to Sir Archibald Grant, he recorded this entry in his *Journal* under date Thursday, 7 May 1761:

'About six we went to church. It was pretty well filled with

A CHOIR-LOFT IN THE EIGHTEENTH CENTURY
'The Orphan' by Sir George Reid (*see Chapter* 14)

'AN ORDINATION OF ELDERS' BY J. H. LORIMER

Shows a 'two-decker' pulpit with precentor's desk, in the nineteenth century (*see Chapter* 17)

such persons as we did not look for so near the Highlands. But
if we were surprised at their appearance, we were more so at their
singing. Thirty or forty sang an anthem after sermon, with such
voices as well as judgment, that I doubt whether they could
have been excelled at any cathedral in England.'

The movement spread to the south. In Edinburgh,
the Town Council, in November 1756, enacted 'that
a master well skilled in the theory and practice of
church music shall be immediately employed to teach
in the city, and that a collection of such of our church
tunes as are most proper to be sung shall be published
and sold at a low price; that schools be opened in
different quarters of the city and taught by precentors
and others best qualified'. A numerous Committee
named by the Council included the names of Lords of
Session, Barons of Exchequer, ministers, burgesses, &c.
Seven classes were opened in the city, under qualified
teachers, one of them a lady. The fee required was
1s. 8d. per month, but the poor were taught gratis,
and half-fees for them were provided from a charitable
fund, on the production of a certificate of necessity
from a minister or an elder, and another certifying that
they were capable of being taught. Practices were to be
weekly. No new tune was to be introduced into public
worship without the permission of the Committee.

Cornforth Gilson, already named as from Durham
Cathedral, was the 'Master' chosen. His Lessons on the
*Practice of Singing, with an addition of the church tunes, in
four parts, and a Collection of Hymns, Canons, Airs and
Catches* (1759) gives no very high conception of his
capacity. But his book, and Bremner's, which preceded

M

it three years earlier, in 1756, *Collections of the Best Church Tunes, in Four Parts,* issued 'by Order of the Committee for improving Church Music in the City of Edinburgh', gave a sufficiently good impetus to the movement for reform for which the time was clearly ripe.

Glasgow also made speed to initiate reform. Indeed it was two days ahead of Edinburgh in appointing an official teacher, Thomas Moore by name. He had already made his mark in Manchester by his teaching, and still more by the publication in two volumes of *The Psalm Singer's Divine Companion,* which proved so popular that a second edition was issued in the same year (1750) as *The Psalm Singer's Compleat Tutor and Divine Companion.* In 1755 he went to Glasgow as precentor of Blackfriars Parish Church, and in 1756 was appointed by the magistrates teacher of the free music in Hutcheson's Hospital. In the same year he published in Glasgow *The Psalm Singer's Pocket Companion, containing great variety of the best English Psalm-Tunes, suited to the different metres in the Scotch Version of the Psalms of David, set in three and four parts, likewise all the tunes that are usually sung in most parts of Scotland; with a plain and easy introduction to Musick.* It was from this book that our well-known tune GLASGOW came. Five years later, in 1761, he issued *The Psalm Singer's Delightful Pocket Companion . . . Illustrated with great variety of Tables, Scales, and Initial Lessons.*

These books began the long and copious stream of Glasgow tune-books which made a commercial proposition, and evidently a profitable one, of supplying music for the choirs which were springing up all over the country.

The barriers were down at last: the long reign of the unassailable Twelve Tunes was at an end, and strains very different from those to which congregations had long been unchangeably accustomed began to be heard in the churches.

Chapter 15

Practice-Verses

WHEN the Reformed order was organized, it became an obligation upon the people each to possess a psalm-book. The *Book of Common Order* was bound up with it, but the name used for the combined book came to be the *Psalm-book*. That was the thing that was prized. It was looked upon as demanding hardly less veneration than the Bible: it held the place in people's minds which is held among Roman Catholics by the Missal and the Breviary; potentially or actually it was their chief book of devotion.

That being so, a remarkable consequence followed. The Psalm-book was held so peculiarly sacred that no irreverence in the use of its words must be permitted. It came to be thought as grave a sin to misuse its words as to take the name of God in vain. Not even the precentor, when practising the two Psalms in which on Sunday he was to lead the people, was at liberty in his private rehearsal to use the sacred words: he must find some other medium for practising his craft. There was nothing sacrosanct about the tunes, but the words were not regarded as permissible for use except in the worship of God. Practising was not thought of as a religious exercise; so practice-verses to serve as substitutes for the purpose had to be found.

In the development of this curious usage, three distinct stages can be traced.

To begin with, because practising for the Sunday services, though not regarded as in itself a religious act, was on the border-line of religion, whatever verses the precentor chose to use must be of a character not inconsistent with the purpose in view. There must be nothing in them, certainly, to trench upon the province of worship: they must not be devotional or religious in character: the name of God must not occur in them; there must be no form of address to Him.

But the verses must be grave in character: the sentiment expressed in them must be morally unimpeachable. As a rule it consisted of 'a blash o' cauld morality', such as characterized Moderate preaching when the time came for that variety of pulpit prelection to reach its desolating ascendancy in the Church.

Typical examples are given by Thomas Bruce, schoolmaster in Edinburgh, at the end of the slender Psalter published by him in 1726, under the title *The Common Tunes, or, Scotland's Music made plain*. At that time, be it remembered, only twelve tunes constituted 'Scotland's Music' for church use, and there were no choirs—the precentor had to lead the singing alone.

Bruce prints seven verses entitled 'Lines for Lettering the Common Tunes', as follows:

I

The Summer's hot, the Winter's cold,
Whose seasons lets us see,
When Youth is gone, and we wax old,
Like Flowers we'll fade and die.

II

One Year begins, another ends,
    Our Time doth pass and go;
And this to our Instruction tends,
    If we would take it so.

III

In prime Time of our Youth we should
    The seeds of Learning sow;
In Harvest of Old Age again
    · The Good thereof we'll know.

IV

The slothful Man yet ne'er attained
    To Honour, Wealth, nor Fame;
But many have by Virtue gain'd
    A long long lasting Name.

V

Since all things formed have an End,
    Nothing but Fame remains:
Happy are they that wisely spend
    Their Years in virtuous Pains.

VI

Our Bodies are but brickle Barks
    Which sweem the Seas of Fame;
And if by Sloth we miss our Aim,
    We'll sink in Seas of Shame.

VII

The blessful Flock I saw on Plain,
    Feeding by Shepherd none:
I had not pass'd a Mile or two
    When up starts the lazy Dron.

This last verse is so halting and inferior to the others that it may be taken to be a precentor's own unskilled and ill-judged venture. The others, which were largely used throughout Scotland, are all borrowed from an obviously ancient poem entitled 'Ane Godlie Instructione for Old and Young', which is found in the *Roxburghe Ballads,* undated, and also in *Extracts from the Commonplace Book of Andrew Melville,* who was Doctor and Master of the Song School of Aberdeen from 1621 to 1640.

Two verses, of a later time, may be given also. One is described as 'flat' (i.e. major), the other 'sharp' (i.e. minor), the latter intended for psalms of a more solemn character.

1. *Major.* Enquire, ye pilgrims, of the way
         That leads to Zion Hill,
    And thither set your steady feet
         With a determined will.

2. *Minor.* Our life contains a thousand strings,
         And dies if one be gone:
    Strange! that a harp of thousand strings
         Should keep in tune so long.

During the choirless period, when the precentor had to lead the singing alone, it was not thought necessary that he should restrict himself to such verses as these that were in common use: he might exercise his own choice. Occasionally that choice resulted in untoward consequences, as a single incident will show.

One precentor in Greenock, John McQuisten by name, was an ardent lover of the old Scots ballads, and was accustomed to indulge his affection for them by

using words from them for his Saturday evening practice of the psalms for the following day. His favourite
ballad was 'Sir Patrick Spens'; its closing stanzas in
particular went well to a common-metre tune.

One of John's vanities was the perfection of his
memory. It was probably not he, but it might have
been, who coined this practice-verse out of his customary boast:

> I'm independent o' a book
>   When psalms are being sung:
> There's no' a psalm within the brods
>   But I hae't on my tongue.

So confident was John in the infallibility of his memory that he scorned the use of the printed words when
leading the congregation, and sang with his eyes shut.
This self-confidence, however, was once his undoing.
One Sunday a portion of Psalm 107 was given out,
beginning at verse 21—the passage describing the
plight of the sailors 'who go to sea in ships, and in great
waters trading be', when 'the stormy tempest' over-
takes them and they are at their wits' end because of
danger. All went well till the end of verse 25 was
reached, with two verses of the prescribed portion still
to come. But at that point the storm in the psalm
suggested to John's mind the storm in 'Sir Patrick
Spens'—not unnaturally, for there is a similarity in the
situation. So instead of lining out verse 26, which describes the reeling ship: 'they mount to heaven, then
to the depths they do go down again', he slipped un-
awares into the lines he had used in his practice the
previous evening:

> O laith, laith were oor guid Scots lords
> To weet their cork-heel'd shoon,
> But lang or a' the play was play'd,
> They wat their hats aboon.

The congregation blindly followed their leader. Some, who had the words before them, looked aghast, but the majority, seeing John with his eyes shut and trusting implicitly in his memory, sang on after him without misgiving. The unconscious precentor, thinking more of his trills and grace-notes than of the words, sang the verse through, and the next one after it:

> And mony was the feather-bed
> That fluttered on the faem,
> And mony was the gude lord's son
> That never mair cam' hame.

Then, though the people knew that something had gone amiss, John sat down in bland content, quite unaware that he had done a thing that would be talked about for half a century after he was in his grave.

The outraged minister got over it in time, and would say to the precentor on the Sunday morning, 'Gi'e us nane o' your ballants the day, na, John.'

Advancing a stage further, here are some examples of practice-verses from Robert Bremner's *Rudiments of Music*, published in 1756: two of his four examples of stanzas of eights and sixes, as he puts it (that is, common metre), and two in stanzas of eights (that is, long metre):

> 1. The Heart, by Music's Force inspir'd
>   With sacred Warmth to glow,
> Is with each gen'rous Passion fir'd
>   And tastes a Heav'n below.

2. Deep on the tender Mind imprest,
   The softer Passions play;
   When Music melts the infant Breast,
   And lights fair Virtue's Ray.

3. The man whose dull internal Sense
   By Music here untouch'd remains,
   In Heav'n shall find full Recompense
   And join the Seraphs' loftiest Strains

4. Who would not join the sacred Lays
   And sing the Eternal's endless Praise?
   On Earth below, in Heav'n above,
   The noblest Tasks are Praise and Love.

In these lines a change of emphasis is to be observed. There is a distinct approach to the forbidden religious note. And the element common to all the verses is the transference of the point of stress from morality to music.

This is due to the remarkable stirring of interest in music in the eighteenth century to which reference is made elsewhere. It became the predominant social interest.

'In vain', wrote Captain Topham in 1774-5, 'may a man of letters, whose want of natural faculties has prevented him from understanding an art from which he could derive no pleasure, endeavour to introduce other matters of discourse, however entertaining in their nature: everything must give place to music. Music alone engrosses every idea. In religion a Scotchman is grave and abstracted, in politics serious and deliberate: it is in the power of harmony alone to make him an enthusiast.'

The old religious strictness was relaxing; there was a general advance in cultural interests. The Church was moving into the period of the Moderates, and the change of emphasis in the very practice-verses was symptomatic of the change.

In 1753 the Choir Movement described in Chapter 14 began. When the new choirs got to work they became very quickly tired of singing the same standard practice-verses over and over again. Complaints about the monotony of them provoked a challenge to the complainers themselves to produce something better. This happened, for instance, at Kinnesswood, Kinross-shire, where Michael Bruce, the Loch Leven poet of pathetic memory, was born. In the summer of 1764 he joined a singing-class in the village, taught by a young man, Buchan by name, who had worked in various towns and heard other tunes sung than 'the standard eight' (FRENCH, DUNDEE, STILT or YORK, NEWTOUN, ELGIN, LONDON, MARTYRS, ABBEY) which formed the entire repertory of the congregation; among the new tunes were ST. DAVID, ST. PAUL, ST. THOMAS, and ST. ANNE. Three of the practice-verses in use were these:

O mother dear, Jerusalem,
   When shall I come to thee?
When shall my sorrows have an end,
   Thy joys when shall I see?

The Martyrs' tune, above the rest
   Distinguished is by fame;
On their account I will sing this
   In honour of their name.

Fair London toun, where dwells the King
   On his imperial throne,
With all his court attending him,
   Still waiting him upon.

The first of these is the opening verse of a hymn popular in Scotland in the seventeenth century and still in use;[1] the others are good examples of the feeble doggerel substituted for the psalms. Buchan, the precentor, knowing that Bruce had a poetic gift, asked him to supply something better. Bruce complied, and furnished these familiar verses of three well-known paraphrases (11, 8, and 18):

O happy is the man who hears Instruction's warning voice.
Few are thy days and full of woe, O man of woman born.
The beam that shines from Zion's hill shall lighten every land.

The question whether Bruce ever finished these pieces or whether John Logan did, lies at the core of the now insoluble Bruce-Logan controversy. Let it suffice to say that here were three successful substitutes for the standard practice-verses of which everyone had grown weary.

But few choirs had Michael Bruces in them. None the less, the manufacture of such substitutes went on: it became a popular amusement. Imagine the situation. Choir-practices introduced a new and delightsome interest into rural social life. That interest was by no means entirely musical. Young people, gathered in from a wide country-side, soon discovered that it was possible to infuse into the practices a good deal of harmless and enjoyable gaiety. The invention of new verses was a rich source of fun.

Sometimes the verse was designed to convey instruction as to the singing:

[1] See note on Hymn 595 in the *Handbook to the Revised Church Hymnary*.

Come, raise your voices loud and clear,
    And keep in proper time;
Then you may cast away your fear
    And sing to any rhyme.

All people that OLD HUNDREDTH sing,
    With cheerful voice this measure take;
Gar ilka line wi' grandeur ring,
    Put on the seventh note a shake.

The names of tunes were immediately suggestive. For example:

Come, let us sing the tune of FRENCH,
    The second measure low;
The third ascendeth very high,
    The fourth doth downward go.

This was the tune the MARTYRS sang
    When they went forth to die,
When on the scaffold they did stand,
    The truth to testify.

ST. DAVID stands wi' hairp in haund:
    He's maister o' the queer (choir);
Ten thousand times that man is blest
    Who doth sic music hear.

ST. PAUL, he was a godly man,
    Although of stature low;
He did the gospel faithful preach
    Wherever he did go.

Far in the north of Scotland stands
    An auld toun ca'd DUNDEE,
From which this tune did tak' its flicht
    An' through the world did flee.

Naturally, the invention of rhymes of this type stimulated the sense of humour. Thus:

> The name o' this tune is called YORK,
>> The reason I don't know;
> They micht as well have called it Cork,
>> Carmarthen or Raphoe.

The old Scottish name for YORK was STILT, suggested by its high-stepping movement; whence this rhyme:

> Come, let us a' tak' up the STILT,
>> And mony cripples be;
> But if oor foot should tak' a stane,
>> Doon to the grund fa' we.

Two rhymes were suggested by the tune BANGOR, as follows:

> O BANGOR's notes are unco high,
>> An' try the lassies sair;
> They pech an' grane an' skirl an' skreich,
>> Till they can sing nae mair.

> The high high notes o' BANGOR's tune
>> Are unco sair to raise;
> An' tryin' hard to reach them gars
>> The lassies burst their stays.

Imagine again the situation when there were pauses in the choir-practices. Here is a rhyme which shows how the interval might be employed:

> Keep silence, all ye sons of men,
>> And hear with reverence due;
> The maister hes gane oot tae smoke,
>> But he'll be back the noo.

At a singing-school at Kirkcowan, Wigtonshire, held in a barn, one lad arrived too late to get his usual seat with the men, and had to sit beside the girls. In the interval some wag made fun of his predicament. He retorted in this verse:

> Though I'm the last, I'm seated best,
>   Among the ladies fair;
> Though standers-by do me en-vý,
>   For that I dinna care.

Once more, imagine the young people making their way homeward in the moonlight along the country roads. What fun they would have in making up such humorous rustic rhymes together! Here is one the first line of which is obviously suggested by 'O mother dear, Jerusalem':

> O mither dear, Tod Lowrie's lum,
>   Whan sweepit will it be?
> For a' the soot's come tummlin' doon,
>   An' spilet ma grannie's tea.

Another from the west of Scotland—Paisley and Ayr-shire—ran:

> A weaver said unto his son
>   The day that he was born,
> My blessings on your curly pow;
>   You'll rin wi' pirns the morn.

Occasionally there was a vein of sentiment in the rhymes:

> The man that climbs where naething hangs
>   And grips where naething grows,
> And loves a maid that loves not him,
>   Against the stream he rows.

> I wish my love was a red rose,
>   Grown in my garden wall,
> And I to be a drope o' dew;
>   Upon her I would fall.

It is easy to understand how of the many vulgar rhymes, those that come nearest to being coarse, and even ribald, originated in circumstances like those described:

> I wish I were a brewer's horse
>   Yoked to a cairt o' yill,
> And that my heid was at my tail;
>   Then I could drink my fill.

Vincent Sheean, in his *Between the Thunder and the Sun*, speaking of the influence of newspaper commentators in America, says that one result of this method of exercising democratic control was that 'Jokes travelled [across the Continent] as if by telepathy or black magic. You heard one in New York one week, and in San Francisco the next; they knew no limits of circulation, even though the best of them were too rude to print.' The same thing was true of the tune-rhymes: the nearer they came to the edge of the permissible, or passed beyond it, the faster they flew from parish to parish. Thus the same almost unbelievably rude rhymes are found in Orkney, and right down the country to the Mull of Galloway. For this kind of thing was going on, as one local record assures us, more or less at every school in Galloway; and that district may be taken to represent what was true all over the country.

No evidence seems to exist, however, that these

crude levities were used in serious practices; they were coined in fun and circulated in the same spirit. And account must be taken of what the Ettrick Shepherd characterized as 'the rude and energetic humour of the Scots'.

In the period to which these rhymes belong that humour was apt to be exceedingly broad. Readers of the old ballads know that well: and the fact that Allan Ramsay and Burns had both to cleanse the Augean stable of the traditional songs to make them fit for decent use, tells its own tale. It may well be that there *were* tune-rhymes coined in fun which were of the same character as the humour of the period; but so far as I know, none such have been preserved in print, or even in memory.

It has to be remembered also that, as Dean Ramsay said, 'There certainly was a quaint and familiar manner in which sacred and solemn subjects were referred to by the older Scottish race, who did not mean to be irreverent, but who no doubt appeared so to a more refined but not really a more religious generation.'

And John Buchan has two relevant things to say which those familiar with the Scottish mind will readily endorse. In one of his Canadian addresses he said to a Scottish audience: 'We are a reverent people, and yet we can be exceedingly free with our sacred things, as anyone who has read half-a-dozen Covenanting sermons will admit. . . . Even in our most serious and solemn moods we have our touches of comedy.' Again, remarking that Scottish poetry is to a great degree a reflex of the Scottish character, he says that

N

it combines within itself startling anomalies. He compares it aptly to some cathedral of the Middle Ages, with peasants gossiping and laughing in the nave, and the devout at prayer in side-chapels; and with carved grotesques adjacent to stained-glass saints.

These rhymes belong to a simpler and ruder age than ours, but they are part of our history. They were never used in their earlier forms except as a safeguard against irreverence, and in their later and lighter forms were the mere froth of young people's social gaiety.

Chapter 16

The Newer Types of Psalm Tunes

IN Scotland, as in England, the early psalm-tunes were in one respect of a single type: they were syllabic, with a single note to each syllable of the words. By virtue of this simplicity, which was at first essential for a people learning an unfamiliar art, tunes of that kind are first in popularity still.

But obviously the syllabic rule meant a severe limitation of musical interest. Music has such endless possibilities of variety that so restricted a usage could not permanently satisfy.

Three ways of increasing the interest were open. One was to enrich the harmonies. That way was taken in due time by Bach in his treatment of the German chorales—to what splendid purpose many examples in modern hymn-books show. Another way was to introduce variety into the rhythm. Bourgeois took that way in the French psalter-tunes; sometimes he varied the rhythm from line to line. How fine the effect was may be judged by comparing the syllabic tune COMMAND-MENTS with Bourgeois's original unspoiled form of it, in the lovely tune LES COMMANDEMENS DE DIEU. The third way was taken in England and Scotland, that of filling in and embellishing the melody itself.

The first step in this last process was that of making a small departure from the convention of one note only to one syllable. The occasional addition of a second note was ventured upon, and the effect was found to be so pleasing that it was ecstatically welcomed. It was of course not a new practice, but a return to the way of the plain-song composers, who grouped notes for single syllables—not two only, but often many more. This new departure in the direction of vitalizing the music of psalmody was first made in the 1708 Supplement to Tate and Brady's New Version of the English Psalter. There, in addition to other great tunes of Dr. Croft, appeared his ST. MATTHEW, one of the most splendid of all the eight-line tunes. It derives much of its attractiveness from its moderate departure from the strictly syllabic form. The example set by the innovation was eagerly followed, with many fine results. What, for example, could be more perfect than WAREHAM, the spacious smoothness of whose conjunct movement is achieved by double notes to a syllable. Many memorable and well-loved tunes were produced by this device —COLCHESTER, ST. STEPHEN, WARRINGTON, to name but three.

A further step in the departure from convention was that of disregarding the rule that no notes but minims and semibreves should be allowed in psalm-tunes. In 1709, in Playford's *Divine Companion*, Jeremiah Clark's revolutionary tune BISHOPTHORPE appeared—a captivating tune, with a fine melodic contour, and a bright grace of spirit impossible to resist. Its charm depends partly on the secondary notes of all kinds Clark attaches to certain syllables, and partly on the rhythmical variety he introduces to enliven the usual unbroken pro-

cession of minims and semibreves. Once this engaging
innovation was accepted, crotchets and quavers multiplied, and even semiquavers were not long in following.

Take, as an early example of the change produced in
this way, the tune BANGOR, of 1734. Sung at a proper
speed, it is a beautiful tune, and its great popularity in
the eighteenth and early nineteenth centuries is not
difficult to understand. But it lent itself easily to being
travestied. Channon marked its character as 'deeply
mournful'; but singers were so delighted with the new
freedom of movement it allowed them after the stiffness
and stateliness of the older tunes, that they ran away
with it: they raced the tune to such an extent as to make
it an offence to people whose affections were wedded
to the old solemnity. Thus it is easy to guess why
Burns, for instance, did not take kindly to it. In *The
Cotter's Saturday Night* he praised DUNDEE, ELGIN, and
MARTYRS, tunes used doubtless in the family worship
of his godly father's household and in the Moderate
churches in Ayrshire with which he was most familiar.
A taste formed upon these grave and slow-moving
tunes was bound to be repelled by the briskness of the
new style which was just coming into use in his youth,
especially if the singers yielded to the temptation to
sing at a break-neck speed. Apparently that was how
he heard BANGOR sung, for in *The Ordination* he says:

> Mak' haste an' turn King David owre,
>   And lilt wi' holy clangor;
> O' double verse come gie us four,
>   An' skirl up 'the Bangor'.

The word 'skirl' is eloquent of the speed and quality of

the new singing; so is the fact that it made it possible to sing double the usual portion of the psalm. Such speed indicates the pit into which much psalm-singing fell—and too often still falls. Tunes of the type in question should be sung at a moderate speed, but there are organists of whom it has been said that a crotchet is to them like the smell of battle; it suggests a rollicking tempo which bids good-bye to devotion. Better not sing such tunes at all than ruin them—and ruin worship at the same time—by singing at so unsuitably rapid a speed.

It was not a musical emancipation alone that accounted for the introduction of livelier tunes. The Evangelical Revival in England in the eighteenth century brought a vivifying breath of new life into the spiritual atmosphere. It created an irresistible demand for joyful hymns and joyous tunes to suit them. Expression had to be found for the sheer exultation of souls that had found the gladness of the new life in Christ, and to supply the need a host of tunes were written. Some of the most characteristic of them are found in our hymnody: for example, HEATON NORRIS to 'O happy day that fixed my choice'; MELLING to 'Let us with a gladsome mind'; and MOUNT EPHRAIM to 'Come, we that love the Lord'. But the new spirit produced psalm-tunes also, such as DOVERSDALE, LIVERPOOL, UNIVERSITY, WARWICK.

From the 'programme' here given of the tunes Channon and his choir sang when they first exhibited their skill in Aberdeen, it will be seen that he made use of some of the finest of the new-style tunes, but also—

he being almost certainly a Methodist—that he was captivated most by the less admirable style.

	Parts	Time	Character	Psalm
Abingdon	3	Common	Cheerful and solemn	90. 1
*C Psalm	3	Common	Cheerful and solemn	100. 1
Zealand	4	Triple	Cheerful and lively	149. 1
Kidderminster	4	Triple	Very cheerful	103. 1
Fintray	3	Triple	Example of great joy	33. 1
*Monymusk	3	Triple	Very cheerful	84. 1
*Paradise	4	Common	Grand and cheerful	98. 1
St. Matthew	3	Triple	Pastoral and lively	23. 1
St. Anne	3	Common	Pastoral expressive of longing	63. 1
Althorpe	3	Common	Solemn	24. 3
Colchester	4	Triple	Lively and grand	150. 1
*Kintore	4	Common	Very grand and cheerful	98. 4
London New or Newton	3	Common	Grand	104. 1
Dundee	3	Common	Complaining	13. 1
Rugby	3	Triple	Melancholy	42. 1
Hartford	4	Triple	Penitential	51. 1
*Rayne	3	Triple	Mournful and supplicatory	102. 1
Bangor	3	Common	Deeply mournful	55. 1

* New Tunes.

The tunes bearing Aberdeenshire place-names and classed as new may be assumed to have been of Channon's own composition. MONYMUSK, unfortunately, will not bear reproduction: it is a 'repeater' of an unmanageable kind. But KINTORE is here given as proof that great as Channon's ability as conductor and propagandist must have been, he had no skill as a composer.

KINTORE.   C.M.   G♯ 3rd.

It will be observed that in Channon's list 'C PSALM' is marked as a new tune, and that ST. MATTHEW is, inappropriately, the tune assigned to Psalm 23.

As the movement Channon initiated spread, and choirs were formed all over the country, tune-books were multiplied, chiefly in Glasgow, as has been already said, but in other widespread quarters also. Long oblong books they were, with two tunes usually to the page. Obviously ill-edited, and competing with each other in the quantity of attractive material they presented, they contained a mixture of the older tunes with many more of the most varying quality, swept up from every quarter. A large proportion of them must have been far beyond the capacity of the choirs, and still more of ordinary people expected to sing them.

The new fluency in style carried tune-writers to great lengths in the period in question. They introduced profusely roulades, runs, repeats, which made the tunes they were intended to adorn much more attractive to the singers than the steady-going syllabic tunes which had palled by incessant repetition and by the slow long-drawn-out dullness of the manner which was thought appropriate in singing them. Their spirited melodic style was at the other extreme from the dreary drawl to which generations had been accustomed.

Decorative writing was carried to an absurd excess, without any consideration frequently of its suitability to the words. Take the following tune CLIFFORD, or VICTORY, written for the 121st Psalm.

So degenerate became the taste of the time that even such dignities as OLD HUNDREDTH were thought to be improved by being defaced with meaningless decorations. Similarly, the frugal outline of TALLIS'S CANON was filled with crotchets until the original tune was buried almost unrecognizably underneath them; then the crime was disguised by giving the result a new name such as BRENTWOOD, or SUFFOLK.

Good un-to all men is the   Lord: O'er all His works His
mer - cy is.   Thy works all praise to   Thee af - ford:
Thy   saints, O   Lord, Thy . . name shall bless.

The repeater tunes, of which the Tunes in Reports had been the precursors, became enormously popular. An example is given on p. 185 in CLIFFORD. Dr. Arnold's NEW LYDIA was for long a special favourite, but its interest was seen to be purely secular the moment any relation was sought for between it and the sacred words to which it was intended to be sung. Many others, which even violated the sense of the words, fell into deserved neglect when they came to be recognized as wellnigh a mockery in association with the worship of God.

For the time being, attractive tunes were sought for everywhere. The oratorios were ransacked for melodies that might be torn from their context and tortured into

the shape of a psalm-tune. 'I know that my Redeemer
liveth' appeared for psalmodic purposes under the
name MESSIAH. Similarly hymn-tunes were pressed
into service. The 'chief favourite' tune of Dr. Chalmers, which the precentor almost every Sunday got
specific instructions to sing to the last act of praise in
services the Doctor conducted, was SCARBOROUGH,
which is a version of MILES LANE, subjected to the
necessary maltreatment to convert it into a psalm-tune.

Secular tunes were rarely requisitioned, as they had
sometimes been in the earliest days of the Reformation;
but some aberrations did occur, as when 'The harp
that once through Tara's halls' was offered as a psalm-
tune under the name HIBERNIA.

Wild guesses were made to provide impressive names
of composers. Thus BURFORD and WALSAL were
attributed to Purcell; and ST. MARY'S and HANOVER
were described as German melodies, the former said to
be by 'Rathiel', the latter alleged to be 'adapted by
Handel'.

Such lavish and undiscriminating assemblages of
tunes from every available quarter naturally bred the
illusion that to write new tunes was no very difficult
matter. In point of fact, few musical ventures are more
unlikely to achieve success. But amateur composers
showed astonishing fertility in producing new tunes
to put into competition with the standard ones, and
publishers were seemingly eager to add these to their
collections. Doubtless among these sanguine aspirants
to distinction there were some at any rate with so
inflated a notion of the quality of their productions as

to feel what one was indiscreet enough to put into expression, in modest deprecation of a too favourable estimate of his tune: 'It may not be very good, but at any rate it is a good deal better than TALLIS.'

Most of these tunes, however popular in their day, have long since gone to oblivion. An attempt to revive some of them in the present century under the alluring but misleading title *Old Scottish Psalm Tunes* had a temporary measure of acceptance. Many of the tunes included were no older than last century; some were not psalm-tunes at all; quite half of them were certainly not Scottish; a good many were English, and a fair number, like BARROW, BOSWELL, and BOYLSTON, were American. In the last class was one arch-deceiver, named COVENANTERS, which imposed itself upon the credulous as a genuine survival from Covenanting times. The few tunes sung in those times are among the most assuredly known things in musical history, and no tune bearing the most distant resemblance to the one in question has any place among them.

This was an interregnum period, when there was no standard to judge by, and no authoritative teacher to give guidance, and the Church itself did nothing to provide what was needed. Few of the tunes produced by amateurs had any chance of surviving. But among those few are some which have a place in general affection. Especial note may be taken of those in the Caledonian or pentatonic scale (five notes to the scale). 'This scale', it has been said, 'is almost a tune in itself, and any order of the notes has beauty.'[1] So many of the

---

[1] *Oxford Companion to Music*, p. 836.

finest Scottish secular tunes are based upon this scale that any psalm-tune using it is almost secure of favour. The same is true of tunes using a six-note scale. Thus MARTYRDOM, KILMARNOCK, MORVEN, DRUMCLOG, STRACATHRO, SELMA, written by amateurs with the exception of the last, which was based on a Highland melody, are so dear to the Scottish heart that some of them tend to be much over-sung. SELMA, and possibly MARTYRDOM also, betoken the modern return to the folk-song tune as a source.

Guides to sound standards of judgement were needed to lead the Church out of the chaos into which it fell in this period. As the nineteenth century advanced, the needed leaders appeared.

Chapter 17

The Era of the Great Precentors

WHEN reform definitely set in, its progress was inevitably slow. Both precentors and people needed to be taught how to sing, and the process in its earlier stages could not be hastened.

In 1746 the General Assembly recommended 'the ancient practice of singing without reading the line'. Yet not till eleven years later did the Kirk Session of St. Machar's, Aberdeen, take advantage of this permission, adopt the practice in public worship, and recommend 'masters of families that they take pains to cause their children and servants to sing the Church Tunes in a regular manner, that they might be able to join most skilfully in this part of public worship'. More astonishing is it that not till twenty years had elapsed—in 1766—was it noted as a subject worthy of remark in Edinburgh that in one of the churches there 'they have begun to sing every Sunday without reading the line'. One congregation in Aberdeen (the Associate Church, now Melville) did not essay any reform until 1830, and even then made no changes that were not reluctant and slight. The 'run-line' was only half abandoned, the decision being in favour of reading out two lines at a time instead of one. And, a group of petitioners having asked that certain specified new tunes should be brought into use as being 'all very decent and becoming the worship of God', the Session agreed that occasionally one of those proposed might be tried. Among the novelties thus grudgingly permitted were IRISH, COLCHESTER, MARTYRDOM, and OLD HUNDREDTH.

One reason for the slowness of advance was undoubtedly the fact that the majority of the members of the new singing classes were incapable of reading music and had to learn by ear: they had enthusiasm but no skill. Bremner betrays this in the illuminating preface to his *Rudiments of Music*. He estimates that, even after what appear to have been daily practices, since he speaks of several lessons occupying a week, his choir will learn only one tune in four parts every week. They ought, he thinks, in twelve weeks to learn twelve tunes, which he accounts a sufficient number for any congregation. The teacher will do well, however, he says, if he does not hurry progress quite so much as that, but masters only twelve tunes in six months. To make this possible, the singers should sit together, 'to save them from confusion', caused apparently by members, isolated from each other, going astray from the tune. As a further safeguard he recommends that all should sing tenor (the melody) for three or four Sundays, and in that time not more than three tunes should be used. Singing in unison should continue until 'the ignorant' (he does not say whether he means in the choir or the congregation) have got a proper grip of the tune; then let them 'shake off' into their own parts. Even after that, they may sing tenor in the first verse, to help the people.

Some light on the situation is shed by Dr. Beattie's

famous Letter, in 1829, to Dr. Hugh Blair, the Edinburgh preacher and rhetorician, on the Improvement of Psalmody. His musical opinions are sometimes wide of the mark. But two defects, to which he drew attention, give us a significant indication of what must have been difficult to endure in the practice of psalm-singing at that time.

'I would earnestly entreat those who sing very ill', he says, 'not to sing at all, at least in the church. If they are silent, they may have their affections raised by the singing of others: but if they sing, especially if they sing loud (which bad singers seldom fail to do) they will not hear the congregation, and they must disturb every person in the neighbourhood of their pew, who has a musical ear. It is a hard case, in performing an act of devotion, to have one's senses confounded and one's thoughts discomposed, by those unmerciful bawlers, whose roarings are generally loud in proportion as they are untuneable.'

He urges also that the psalms should be sung with such distinctness that they who are hearers may understand the words pronounced by the singers. 'For were this rule observed, that excessive drawling would be avoided which tends rather to stupefy than to elevate the mind; and pious sentiments and harmonious sounds would naturally enliven and recommend each other.' It is related that a minister from England visiting Scotland and hearing for the first time this kind of slow drawling singing to the 100th Psalm, which calls upon the people to 'sing to the Lord with cheerful voice', said afterwards, 'If this is your joy, what can be your lamentation?'

These faults of bawling and drawling appear to have been very common. And they explain the policy of

R. A. Smith, the first of the great race of precentors to bring about a change. Although of Scottish parentage, he was born and brought up in England, and retained the English style of speech all his life. In 1807 he became precentor of Paisley Abbey, and his coming to Scotland has been said—and there is no exaggeration—to have marked the beginning of a new era in the music of the Scottish Church. He appears to have realized that the only way of ending the discordant bawling and drawling was to tone down and subdue the singing of the people by refining the singing of the choir. He devoted himself to choir-training, and made his choir-practices so attractive that listeners crowded to hear them, till admission had to be given by ticket.

The fame of the singing in the Abbey spread, and people came from far and near to hear it. The formation of an Abbey Harmonic Choir led to the giving of a series of recitals of a kind without precedent in the west of Scotland. The choir was superbly trained, and sang with instrumental accompaniment. John Fraser of Newfield, writing of the first recital he attended, said:

'Several of (Smith's) own anthems were sung, and the Hallelujah Chorus, and the Chorus of Angels from Beethoven's *Mount of Olives*, with some of the classical choruses. I had never heard sacred music other than simple psalm tunes. The effect on me was transcendently overpowering. I was in an agony of delight; my whole nervous system was trembling and kindling with emotions no language could describe. That was a revelation of heavenly music entirely new to me.'

Before Smith left Paisley, a newspaper of the time

o

remarked that he 'turned the singing of the Abbey band to soft and feeling music from what was drawling, harsh, and noisy'; and according to the managers of the Abbey Music Fund, he brought the Psalmody to 'a state of perfection hitherto unknown in Scotland'.

The effect produced upon the congregation, however, was to reduce them almost to silence: the singing was left largely to the precentor and the choir. One obstinate old woman refused to be put to silence and persisted in bearing her part. Remonstrances with her were useless. 'Na, na,' she said, 'she would not be silent, but would praise the Lord wi' a' her micht, whether she kent the tune or no.' Tradition has it that it was partly to escape from this spoiler of the musical feast that Smith resolved to accept the call to Edinburgh. His departure ended the attractive power of the Abbey musical service. A successor, Andrew Thomson, in his preface to *Paisley Abbey Congregational Psalmody* (1850), says that although the admirers of Sacred Music were in Smith's time drawn from all parts of Scotland 'to listen to its fine flow of devotional psalmody . . . unfortunately the singing of the Band (choir) became gradually a matter of musical display, and the congregational singing, if not discouraged, has been generally neglected, so that it is long since the Abbey congregation, in a great measure, have ceased to sing'.

Smith's Paisley triumph was repeated when he went to St. George's, Edinburgh, in 1823 as leader of psalmody under the direction of the like-minded Dr. Andrew Thomson. He did still more there to rescue Scottish Psalmody from 'the barbarism and degeneracy into which it had fallen throughout the parishes of the country'. Successive collections of psalm-tunes, in which the two men co-operated, culminating in *The Sacred Harmony of the Church of Scotland,* did much to extend the influence for good of the colleagues in St. George's.

Anyone who examines these collections will be struck by several things: (1) the small extent to which the tunes of the old Scottish psalmody are drawn upon; (2) the ill-judged use of melodies 'culled from the great masters' (the oratorios); (3) the considerable infusion of repeating tunes, then in great vogue, and the acceptance of the type by the editors in tunes of their own which remain popular in spite of their belonging to a variety of 'period' tunes now fallen from favour; (4) the introduction of short anthems under the name of sanctuses and doxologies, to be sung by the choir at the end of the services; and (5) the large mortality among the tunes written by the editors themselves. Thomson's ST. GEORGE'S EDINBURGH is high in favour still; his REDEMPTION is still printed but little sung, and Smith's INVOCATION remains in constant use. These may be described as anthem-tunes. For the rest, Thomson's eleven tunes are now completely forgotten; and only Smith's SELMA and MORVEN, both of folk-tune origin, and his vigorous ST. LAWRENCE and less vital ST. MIRREN retain their places in use. Of Smith's compositions in general, George Hogarth, author of a *History of Music,* said the just thing in the *Edinburgh Courant* after Smith's too early death:

'His compositions partake of the character of his mind; they are tender and generally tinged with melancholy, simple and unpretending, and always graceful and unaffectedly elegant. He had not the advantage of a regular musical education or of having his taste formed on the classic models of the art. But there was in his mind a native delicacy and an intuitive soundness of judgment. He had the admirable good sense to know how far he could penetrate into the depths of counterpoint and modulation without losing his way.'

After Smith's day there was a period when precenting was regarded as a fine art, and outstanding practitioners of it were centres of attraction. Edinburgh had three notable examples—John Templeton of Broughton Place Church, John Wilson of St. Mary's, and David Kennedy of Nicolson Street, father of Mrs. Kennedy Fraser. The first two forsook precenting for the stage, and had much success as operatic tenors. Kennedy chose rather the concert platform, and became a popular exponent of Scottish song on both sides of the Atlantic.

On one occasion when Templeton returned to Edinburgh to sing in opera, he called on his old minister, the venerable Dr. John Brown of Broughton Place. 'You must give us a day at the desk', Dr. Brown said, and Templeton assented. The rumour that he was to precent brought a great throng to an always crowded church. One of the psalms to be sung was set to Croft's tune ST. MATTHEW. The singing had not proceeded far when the congregation ceased to take part; they listened to the golden voice which was ostensibly leading them. When the end of the allotted portion of the psalm was ended, Dr. Brown leant over the pulpit desk, and said, 'Just go on, John, just go on.' How long John went on the story does not tell us.

These three men were so notable in their day that they were commemorated together by a bronze plaque on the rock of the Calton Hill, above the steps ascending from Waterloo Place, bearing their heads and names and nothing more. The memorial must be an enigma now to many who pause to look at it, for all three are virtually forgotten. They won their fame only as vocalists; none of them was in any sense a reformer. And the need of the time was for leadership in the reform of congregational singing.

Three names deserve specially honourable mention among those who advanced the cause of good psalmody. The first, German by birth, Joseph Mainzer, had a genius for infusing his own ardent delight in music into large classes of working people. For five years (1842–7) he lived in Edinburgh, and also toured the country, lecturing and teaching. He was an enthusiastic and skilful teacher, and really taught the multitude to sing. Not the least of his services was his publication in 1845 of his *Standard Psalmody of Scotland*, in the preface to which he remonstrates with the Scottish people for their neglect of the musical treasures in the Psalter of the Scottish Reformation—that of 1564. A number of these forsaken treasures he included in his book.

The next to be honourably mentioned is Thomas Legerwood Hately, who was the first precentor of the Free Church General Assembly. By classes he conducted in Edinburgh, and by what he called 'Aggregate Meetings' at Assembly time, he so proved his gifts as

teacher and lecturer that the Assembly sent him out
on a mission of musical instruction throughout the
country. He attracted and taught huge classes—500,
600, and in Greenock 900. And he really taught them,
and interspersed his teaching with historical and
critical remarks on the tunes sung, which were prepared with great care and remarkable accuracy considering the state of musical scholarship at that time.
His aim was an advance upon R. A. Smith's: it was not
at choir singing, but at singing by the congregation.
That was what now called most urgently for reform.
The *Scottish Guardian* of May 1848 said: 'The instances
of ignorance and bad taste to which the ear is bound to
listen in church singing are innumerable. Some shout
at the utmost pitch of their voices—some wheeze with
their breath—some sing through their nose, others
with clenched teeth.' Four years later, in May 1852,
The Witness (Hugh Miller's paper) pronounced an even
more emphatic judgement: 'The combined screams of
a whole congregation, all driving at the air, formed
a compound of villainous sound, and scientifically a
breach of every law of harmony.'

Hately's endeavour to remedy this state of things
was powerfully furthered in the north-east by the
independent work of William Carnie. In 1854 Carnie
gave a memorable lecture in Aberdeen, to 2,000 people,
on Psalmody in Scotland. Its effects were far reaching.
One result was that in the following year the General
Association for the Improvement of Psalmody was
formed. Elementary classes were organized for the
study of music; also a large class under Carnie's direc-

tion for the practice of tunes from *The People's Tune Book*
and other sources. This class, at various stages, numbered from 500 to 700 and 900 members, old and young.
The effectiveness of his teaching may be estimated from
the following remarkable fact. When in 1857 the Rev.
John Curwen visited Aberdeen to propagate his new
Tonic Sol-fa system, a crowded audience of people
interested in psalmody were subjected to a test in
reading music at sight. A slip with a printed long-
metre tune not known to them was distributed. When
Carnie gave the keynote, 'the audience rose *en masse*,
and in a trice the four parts, treble, alto, tenor, bass,
were ringing forth from every quarter of the hall.
Mr. Curwen was greatly pleased, and complimented
the meeting by saying that it was very much like
carrying coals to Newcastle for him to come to Aberdeen and teach a large body to sing at sight.'

In 1870 Carnie formed the Choir of the Thousand
Voices. Weekly meetings were held on what was called
'a gigantic scale'. Ardent lovers of congregational
praise drove miles to take part in these practices. The
music practised was mainly psalm- and hymn-tunes,
with short easy anthems. In the end 'it was glorious
when the whole multitude, choir and audience—say
a couple of thousand singers'—joined in the common
praise.

In two respects Hately and Carnie did necessary and
notable service.

In the first place, they firmly discountenanced the
repeating and other meretricious tunes which overspread the country like a flood, through the Glasgow

tune-books which were in wide use in the first half of
the century. Carnie involved himself in controversy by
saying plainly: 'Glasgow, by its publications in this
line, has done more to vitiate public taste for congregational singing than any other town in the land'. The
tunes he assailed were MERKSWORTH, ST. MARNOCK'S,
LAIGH COMMON, VIOLET GROVE, and others contained
in the three books—*Brown Robertson's*, *Cameron's*, and
Mitchison's—which at that time held the affection of the
western choirs and precentors against all others. He
was 'hit hard and straight' by anonymous opponents.
In reply, he challenged his foes to join him in submit-
ting the tunes in question to Church musicians of
authority like Havergal, Horsley, Sebastian Wesley,
and Gauntlett. 'The rest was silence': no one took up
the challenge. And the tunes in question disappeared
from the pages of later Psalters.

Hately also bent all his efforts towards displacing
these unworthy tunes and replacing them by the great
standard tunes and others of the same quality. How
great his success was may be judged by this quotation
from the columns of *The Witness* in 1852:

'Two or three years ago the model tunes were held to be those
most secular in their melodic structure and harmony, and distinguished by a couple of sentimental repeats, mangling alike
the words and the worship. . . . The taste has turned, and now
runs in a more healthy channel. . . . We read in the change the
early doom of all the ranting Pietys, New Lydias, and Auburns;
the vulgar Sheffields and Gainsboroughs; the insipid Carolines
and Arabias, and the diddle-dawdle Pembrokes, Devizes, and
Hamiltons; and welcome the rise and popularity of the old
unfading school, which claims French, Gloucester, York, and

St. Mary's as its own. And to this desirable end nothing more contributed than Mr. Hately's work, *The National Psalmody*.'

Tribute of the same kind ought equally to be paid to Carnie.

The second outstanding service both rendered was that of editing and publishing standard Psalters which greatly helped to raise and steady the level of congregational singing. Hately's *Free Church Psalmody* in 1844 was followed in 1848 by *The National Psalmody*, to which was added 'A Short and Easy Practical Guide to Psalm Singing'. Carnie began in 1859 by issuing *Fly-Leaves of Hymn and Psalm Tunes*—four-page penny sheets each containing seven tunes old and new. In one of them CRIMOND first appeared. These were circulated in thousands, and ultimately in collected form composed *The Northern Psalter*, which for long years was unchallenged as the standard tune-book in the north-east.

The work of men like Hately and Carnie could not have met with such marked success in churches so obstinately determined to remain unprogressive, unless it had been assisted by outside favourable influences.

One of these was derived from the general advance in musical interest and culture, alike in town and country. Thus Stark, in his *Picture of Edinburgh* in 1806, said: 'Perhaps at no period in the annals of Scottish music was this art more universally cultivated than at present. It forms a part of modern education, and few are to be met with who cannot sing or play upon one instrument or another.' This was the more remarkable because the country was passing through a period of financial strain consequent upon the continental wars,

which adversely affected every kind of aesthetic culture. The rise of the New Town in Edinburgh also
ended the usefulness of St. Cecilia's Hall as the musical
centre of the city. But better times were at hand. The
organization of Musical Festivals, which had for their
scene the Parliament Hall and the Theatre Royal, set
flowing the currents of renewed activity in 1815, 1819,
and 1824. An Edinburgh Professional Society of Musicians did incalculable service by sending parties of
instrumentalists to Dundee, Aberdeen, and other
places to assist local enthusiasts in nourishing music in
their areas. In Glasgow the Sacred Music Institution,
founded in 1796, held weekly rehearsals and gave six
public concerts every season, the programme consisting of psalm-tunes, anthems, and solos. A tendency to
monotony in the fare it provided abated public interest
and brought it to an end. But the first sixteen years of
the nineteenth century have been called 'The Precentors' Period', owing to the formation of a Union of
Precentors who taught classes, gave performances with
their own people, and organized public concerts besides. About the middle of the century Choral Societies
began to spring up all over the land. The work they
did was of quite extraordinary value.

The progress which this indicates was much facili-
tated by the widespread use of Curwen's Tonic Sol-fa
system. Though often depreciated by musical purists,
this system made sight-reading and effective singing
possible for multitudes to whom the staff notation
presented a closed door. And it has been well said that
though the Tonic Sol-faists were rarely cultured

musicians they 'were practical working psychologists, basing all their methods upon actual experience in the art of grading their instruction by steps so small as to offer no obstacle'. Country choirs, and good singing in country churches, became possible when this new system came into use. The evils of singing 'by ear' and of indifference to guidance began to become mere memories.

Perhaps the most effective means of producing order and harmony, and eliminating abuses, was the publication by the Churches of official Psalters. For a considerable time, it is true, tunes of the unworthier sort lingered on in these books; but taste was gradually weaned from them.

The Psalter of 1929, now in use, still retains some of the less admirable relics of the past, the 'vulgar SHEFFIELD' for example; but it marks a welcome return to the better elements in our tradition, and particularly to those tunes which follow the Reformation style. Of that style Havergal says that it is 'the only suitable style for large and mixed congregations', and of the tunes so set he says:

'Simple and easy in their phrases, and always syllabic in their partition, the commonest ear and the least cultivated voice could master them. But, simple and easy as they are, they never are vulgar, insipid, or boisterous. Grave but cheerful, dignified and chaste, they are admirably adapted to meet a great variety of language, and to foster a calm and earnest devotion. One test of their excellence, and of their artistic fitness for Church use is the fact that, little as flippant and self-willed singers may like them, all persons of sober taste and devout feelings delight in them.'

And, it may be added, there are no tunes that so completely give voice and fervency to the devotion of Scottish hearts.

When to these are added the best tunes of earlier and later periods, there is in the 1929 Psalter an ample choice of music fitted for use with psalms of every kind and mood.

In one respect the committee responsible for this Psalter made an innovation which is still imperfectly understood—in the introduction into the music of descant and fauxbourdon arrangements. The use of such devices was familiar to the sixteenth century; it caused no difficulty when the mass of the people who sang confined themselves to the tune, which was then in the tenor part; relatively few voices sang the ornamental parts around the melody. Nowadays the full strength of the choir is apt to be concentrated upon descant or fauxbourdon and the tune is either drowned or distinguished with difficulty. The consequence is that the people, seeking to bear their part, are disconcerted and annoyed, with fatal consequences to the worship. Not all the choir, but a select small body of them, should be instructed to 'festoon the melody' with the ornamental accompanying melody or parts, and to do it so lightly as not to drown the normal tune which all the people as well as the rest of the choir should be asked to sing. The revival of a practice which was given up when the 1564 Psalter went out of use should be done with the most solicitous care that it may achieve the delightful effects it is intended to produce.

The editing of the music of this Psalter was entrusted to the competent and safe hands of Dr. T. C. L. Pritchard.

A liberal provision of Indexes makes the book easier to use intelligently and fittingly than any previous Psalter placed at the service of the Church.

IV

The Insufficiencies of the Scottish Psalter

Chapter 18

Attempts to enlarge the Scope of Psalmody

VERY early in the Reformation period it became evident that the restriction of the Church's praise to the contents of the Hebrew Psalter was drawn too narrowly. In the Genevan Psalter two exceptions were allowed. One to us seems extraordinary: it was the Ten Commandments. The other was Simeon's Song, the *Nunc dimittis*, which was permitted because it was sung in the French Church at the close of Communion. These were set to two of Bourgeois's melodies, the first available to us as the perfect setting to 'The day Thou gavest, Lord, is ended'; the second, enhanced by an arrangement of Goudimel's, in *The Church Anthem Book*, to Robert Bridges' 'O gladsome light, O grace, Of God the Father's face'.

In the first Scottish Psalter, in 1564, there were no such additions to the psalmody. But Bassandyne's 1575 Psalter had five; and later Psalters increased the number until in 1635 there were fourteen, namely: The Ten Commandments from the Genevan of 1536; the Prayer after the Commandments, the Songs of Mary and Simeon, the Lord's Prayer, and the Beliefe, from the English Psalter of 1560; the Veni Creator, the Humble Sute of a Sinner, the Complaint of a Sinner, Two Lamentations, and a Thanksgiving, from the

P

English of 1562; with the Song of Moses and a Spiritual Song ('What greater wealth'), which are not found elsewhere.

No tunes were set to them, but references to tunes were given, so that they might be sung if desired. But there is no evidence that they were sung publicly, and it is reasonable to infer that they were intended for private use, in devotion or for instruction.

This inference is supported by the following extract from Calderwood's record of an overture to the General Assembly in 1608: 'That it be of new enacted, that all ministers examine young children of the age of six yeeres, and try that they have the Lord's Prayer and Articles of Beliefe with the Commandments. In the which their parents sall be holdin to instruct them before the said yeeres, together with some form of Grace before and after meate, as also some short morning and evening prayer.' It is probable that the reference is to the versified forms of these documents.

There are signs here of at least the dawn of a recognition that there were other subjects of praise which required to be provided for besides those in the Hebrew Psalms. Two hymns are from the New Testament. As time went on, it was bound to be felt to be necessary to draw more from that source. The limitation of the Church's praise to the lyrics of a pre-Christian era, and the impossibility, imposed by an exclusive use of the Psalter, of Christian people using the name of Christ in their worship-song at all, would in time be felt to be intolerable.

Two centuries were still to be traversed before that

degree of enlightenment was to be reached; but meantime it was something that the first step in that direction was taken. When the General Assembly of 1647
decided that a new version of the Psalter should be
prepared, it gave explicit instructions that a supplement to it, like that of 1635, should be undertaken also.
It resolved that Zachary Boyd, a notable Glasgow
churchman of the time, with an unresting pen and a
high idea of his powers, should 'be at the pains to translate the other Scripturall Songs in meeter, and to
report his travels to the Committee of Assembly' for
consideration by Presbyteries in the following year.
Anyone who has examined Zachary Boyd's copious
effusions of religious verse—*The Psalms of David in
Meeter* (1646) or *The Garden of Zion* (1644)—will be
thankful that a man so well-intentioned but so completely devoid of the essential gift for what was necessary, should have been prevented from fulfilling his
commission. He did his best; he revised and reprinted
his already published versions in 1648; but apparently
he failed to satisfy the Committee. None the less, his
failure should not obscure the significant fact that the
omission from the Psalter of 1650 of a supplement of
Scriptural Songs was so far from being deliberate that
it was contrary to the Assembly's clear and declared
intention. If the work had been committed to more
capable hands, the provision of a collection of Paraphrases might have been anticipated by well over a
hundred years, and a long-standing subject of controversy would have been settled without dispute.

Such a supplement had, for the time, to be omitted.

But the desire for an extension of the Psalmody persisted. For nearly a century it grew; but not till 1741 was a Committee of Assembly appointed to take action. Its first publication of forty-five versions of Holy Scripture in 1745 met with difficulties arising from the political upheaval of that year, but the chief cause of its non-acceptance was, it is understood, that the Moderates, then dominant in the Church, thought the collection too evangelical. The matter was delayed for nearly forty years, but in 1781 the *Translations and Paraphrases, in verse, of several Passages of Sacred Scripture*, known to us now simply as *The Paraphrases*, met the immediate need. Most of the contents are now dead, without hope of resurrection, but included with them are a number of hymns of high rank, which have found their place among the permanent treasures of the Church's song.

In the early years of the nineteenth century, pressure upon the Assembly continued for a further extension of the materials of praise, and in 1807 a new Committee was appointed, with Sir Henry Moncrieff as Convener, to attempt a further improvement upon the Church's Psalmody by 'enlarging the Collection of Translations and Paraphrases from Sacred Scripture'. The discussion of what should be done continued for many years. The Committee was a large one, and included so many prominent names as to excite surprise at the slender results effected by their labours: at least three selections of what was called *Additional Psalmody* were submitted to the General Assembly and printed by their order 'for the inspection of Presbyteries'. The dates of these were 1811, 1814, and 1820. The last of them contained thirty-two psalm-versions, seventeen other versions, of which four were from the Old Testament, and two doxologies.

It would seem that the Committee interpreted its instruction as involving a fresh handling of the existing Metrical Psalms. The reception of such a suggestion was highly discouraging. The Ettrick Shepherd, invited, as he put it, to 'new-versify a part of the Psalms', astonished Principal Baird, who had become Convener of the Committee, by the characteristic vehemence of his reply. He declared that the Principal might as well propose to him to burn his Bible or renounce his religion. 'No, no, Dr. Baird,' he remonstrated, 'for the love of God and your fellow-men have no hand in such an experiment! Our country communities would be less shocked, and their religious rites less degenerated, by the introduction of the liturgy at once, than by a new psalmody.'

Sir Walter Scott used more reasonableness than Hogg did in opposing the project. He pleaded his own incapacity for the task in which Dr. Baird invited him to bear a share. For one thing, he said, he had no acquaintance with 'the original language of Scripture'.

'"Besides," he added, "after all, I am not sure whether the old-fashioned version of the Psalms does not suit the purposes of public worship better than smoother versification and greater terseness of expression. The ornaments of poetry are not perhaps required in devotional exercises. Nay, I do not know whether, unless used very sparingly and with great taste, they are altogether inconsistent with them. The expression of the old metrical translation, though homely, is plain, forcible, and intelligible, and very often possesses a rude sort of majesty which perhaps would be ill exchanged for more elegance. Their antiquity is also a corresponding influence upon the feelings. They are the very words and accents of the early reformers[1] sung by them in woe, in the fields, in the churches, and on the scaffold. The parting with this very association of ideas is a serious loss to the cause of devotion, and scarce to be incurred without the certainty of corresponding advantages. But if these recollections are valuable to persons of education, they are almost indispensable to the edification of the lower ranks, whose prejudices do not permit them to consider as the words of the inspired poetry the versions of living or modern poets, but persist, however absurdly, in identifying the original with the ancient translation.

"I would not have you suppose that I by any means disapprove of the late very well chosen Paraphrases. But I have an old-fashioned taste in sacred as well as prophane poetry. I cannot help preferring even Sternhold and Hopkins to Tate and Brady, and our own metrical version to both. I hope, therefore, that they will be touched with a lenient hand." '

We may assume that this kind of reasoning had more weight with the Committee than the Ettrick Shepherd's indignant bluster. At any rate their ardour in pursuing their project was cooled. Sir Walter's letter was written in 1818, and after the Assembly's disapproval of the 1820 selections submitted to them, the idea of renovating the Psalms was departed from.

But Dr. Baird was determined to achieve some positive result, and under his leadership a new approach to the problem was tried. In 1824 a new and highly influential Committee was appointed. Its line of action

[1] Here Sir Walter was mistaken, for the Reformation Psalter was superseded in 1650. But his intention was to emphasize the sentiment which ought properly to be associated, in connexion with the Psalms, with the memory of the generations gone.

is indicated in a letter of that year addressed by Dr. Baird to Joanna Baillie, at that time eminent as a poetess and dramatist:

'The present copy [i.e. version] of the Psalms is meant to be left entirely untouched and will stand as it is. It would not indeed be proper to touch it. The feelings of the people would, too, revolt against any change as unhallowed and impious. The new Collection, like the former one [that is, of Paraphrases], is merely intended to give a greater opportunity to an officiating Clergyman of selecting subjects of Psalms more suited often to the subject of his Discourse than he can at present command. At the same time, when the old version of the Psalms seems to admit of improvement, much improvement might be made by a new version which would take its place among the other new Translations and Paraphrases.'

The idea now, therefore, was that which is carried out in modern hymnbooks, where many noble alternative versions of Psalms appear as hymns.

The line chosen for the new adventure seems now, to us, extraordinary. Every living poet of any reputation was invited to submit paraphrases of Scripture passages. The net was cast very wide. Thomas Campbell, Wordsworth, Southey, Dean Milman, Mrs. Hemans, Tom Moore, Mrs. Grant of Laggan, and James Montgomery were among those approached. Montgomery generously put all his published compositions at the Committee's disposal—unfortunately in vain. The best of the others pleaded inadequacy for the task proposed to them, and when *they* refused, contributions from the lesser celebrities offered poor compensation.[1]

[1] The present writer has examined the correspondence and contribu-

The youngest member of the Committee, it would seem, was commissioned to approach Scott again, and did so in a highly persuasive way. This was Charles McCombie of Tillyfour. The tenor of his letter gave Scott the impression that the Committee were still cherishing the idea of altering the existing metrical version. In June 1827 Scott wrote to young McCombie urging various reasons why the Kirk of Scotland should be 'very cautious of laying aside or even undervaluing their own ancient translation of the psalms.'

"'It is," he said, "in some cases, perhaps, bald and rude considered as rhythmical composition, but I am very doubtful whether even the rudeness of its literal simplicity does not make it more fit for the purposes of devotion than the affectation of a more ornate version. The spirit of devotion in which these psalms ought to be used should be animated with the sentiment and purpose of worship too much, to be anxious in requiring the frivolous ornaments of poetical art, and in my opinion [is] more likely to be disturbed than enhanced by such garnishing. . . .

"But there is still another argument in favour of the old psalmody, and it is with me a decisive one. . . . The psalms of the old version are those used by the Fathers of our Church to express their sorrows and their triumphs, their hopes and fears, their prayers in danger, and their gratitude for deliverances. This ought to make them invaluable, and with my consent not a line of them should be altered. . . .

"I hope, therefore, the zeal of the General Assembly will pause before they alter the public worship in such an essential point, and if they do not, I will venture to prophesy that, making the best exertions they can, and getting the best assistance, they will not produce a version superior to that now in use, in a different degree than Tate and Brady are superior to Sternhold

tions in the National Library. See his article on 'Scottish Paraphrases: a Forgotten Episode' in *The Church Service Society's Annual* for 1942.

and Hopkins. And in order to gain this very questionable advantage, they will break a hundred devotional associations by which men's minds are invincibly bound to the present version."'

Sir Walter was in favour of an increase in the number of paraphrases, either of particular psalms or of other passages in Scripture. He even asked Dr. Baird to specify passages on which he might try his skill as paraphraser. But Dr. Baird failed to comply with his request, and from that fact we may reasonably infer that he was already aware that the new line on which he had been adventuring led nowhere. The amended scheme had to be abandoned: it passed silently, and fruitlessly, into oblivion.

The truth is that young McCombie was the only member of the Committee who had any perception of the direction in which they ought to have been travelling. 'The pieces I would have', he wrote, 'should, breathing the Spirit, be informed by the simple yet sublime language of Scripture. I know of no volume compiled in modern times that approaches so near as Bishop Heber's', and he was eager to borrow liberally from that source. But even *he* did not clearly see the right track. He was hypnotized, as they all were, by the idea that what was needed was 'devotional poetry', and, in common with the rest of the Committee, he did not realize that the real need was for a book of Christian hymns for use in public worship as a supplement to the Psalms. The material they collected consisted entirely of mediocre religious verse quite unsuitable for singing. Much of it was of the same character as the dullest of the existing Paraphrases, and while the best of it might have been found mildly edifying by a spiritually minded reader, it was as little fitted for use in public worship as most of the Paraphrases are recognized to be to-day. The Committee's wrong point of view was clearly shown by their shaping their course straight for contributors who had none but their poetic talents to qualify them for what they were expected to do, and who also themselves—from Wordsworth and Scott downwards—exposed this fundamental blunder, by protesting their spiritual unfitness for the task.

The Committee were turning their faces the wrong way. With Heber's, Montgomery's, and doubtless also Milman's fine hymns before them, the right course should have been plain. Moreover, one of the smaller disjoined branches of the Scottish Church—the Relief —the most liberal of all the component sections of the now reunited Church of Scotland—had as early as 1794 published a hymnbook—the first in Scotland to do so; and even at the very time when the Church of Scotland Committee were fumbling ineffectually at their business, the Relief Church had in preparation a second hymnbook which, for its time, was of real excellence. But the plain fact is that the 1781 Paraphrases, instead of serving as a stepping-stone towards the Church's adoption of Christian hymns, operated as a barrier in the way of any movement in that direction; for the non-evangelical part of them—the dead part now— was set up as the model to be followed, and as a consequence the whole enterprise was doomed. Owing to this fatal error, the long-drawn-out labour of Dr. Baird and his coadjutors came to nothing: it ended, not only without any positive result, but even without any explicit record of its failure.

The Secession Church followed the example of the Relief by initiating the preparation of a book of hymns, which appeared in 1852, after these two Churches had combined to form the United Presbyterian Church. The Church of Scotland followed with *The Scottish Hymnal* in 1870, and the Free Church with *Psalm Versions, Paraphrases and Hymns* in 1873, followed by *The Free Church Hymn Book* in 1882. Thus, at long last, the many energizings of the Church, in its endeavours to provide a Christian supplement to the Metrical Psalms, began freely to move towards the ever larger enrichment of the Church's praise by the combination of old and new, Hebrew and Christian, psalms and hymns, in which the Church rejoices to-day.

Chapter 19

Literary Defects

IT is long since critical voices were first heard, complaining of the shortcomings of the literary form of
the 1650 Psalter and urging that measures should be
taken to give it a literary polish more consonant with
the requirements of modern taste.

Early in the nineteenth century, Scottish men of
letters were deeply uneasy about the Scottish idiom
and flavour of their style. Broad Scots was still the
common speech even in cultivated circles, but the use
of it was fast turning into a reproach. Distinguished
writers were becoming frankly ashamed of it. Adam
Smith, of *The Wealth of Nations*, lamented that he had
'the misfortune to write in the language of the most
stupid and factious barbarians in the world'. Principal
Robertson, of the University of Edinburgh and leader
of the General Assembly, whose speech was so broadly
Scottish that London society had difficulty in understanding it, got two English friends to read his books
critically, to remove from them what he called his
colloquial barbarisms.

Dr. James Beattie of Aberdeen, the author of *The
Minstrel*, who was hailed in England, though never in
his own country, as a major poet, had a complete con-
tempt for the Scots tongue: he called it vulgar, and
drew up and published a list of Scotticisms to be
scrupulously avoided by educated men. He published

also a persuasive plea for a revised version of the Scottish Metrical Psalms, in order to purge them of the ruggednesses, the obsolete quaintnesses of expression, and the crudenesses of versification which some people with a defective sense of history still find disturbing to their sensibilities.

Beattie's plea gained strength from the fact that England had produced a new version of the kind he desiderated. It was popularly known as Tate and Brady's, from its two Irish authors' names. In it these authors used a lyrical freedom which Beattie knew Scotland would never consent to, but produced a polished and pleasing smoothness of versification such as could not give offence to the most sensitive eighteenth-century literary proprieties. All he pleaded for was the amendment of what did offend refined taste. For notwithstanding all its defects, he considered the Scottish version the best. 'The numbers, it is true,' he said, 'are often harsh and incorrect; there are frequent obscurities, and some ambiguities in style; the Scotch idiom occurs in several places, and the old Scotch pronunciation is sometimes necessary to make out the rhime. Yet [he admitted] in this version there is a manly, though severe, simplicity, without any affected refinement; and there are many passages so beautiful, as to stand in no need of amendation.' He thought that a new version should be compiled from the best passages of former translations, 'with such amendments of the style and measure as may be required to give the whole an appearance of uniformity'. This urgent plea for revision had no apparent effect.

In the following year (1830) a much more detailed and searching criticism was directed upon the Psalter by William Tennant, a very remarkable man, author of the racy mock-heroic poem *Anster Fair*, and subsequently Professor of Oriental Languages in St. Mary's College, St. Andrews. In two articles in the *Edinburgh Literary Journal*, he complained that the Scottish Version, though 'so majestically simple, [is] yet disfigured so largely with pseudo-rhymes, double-rhymes, and no-rhymes—so spotted with violations of ordinary grammar, vicious accentuations, and vulgar Scotticisms, that moderation of praise and dispraise can scarcely be preserved'.

Tennant, however, admitted that many of the Psalms 'are in whole or in part, excellently executed, and considering the difficulty that attends the combination of rhyme with sublimity in that narrow species of couplet to which they are restricted, they may be considered as the finest specimens we have in our language of sublime rhyming translation. Milton himself, in the few psalms he has attempted to translate, has attained by no means their ease and hardly their elevation.' Tennant's plea, like Beattie's, had no positive effect.

The next attempt at improvement was made officially by the Free Church General Assembly in 1866. Full account was taken by the Assembly's Psalmody Committee of the defects against which Tennant directed his criticisms—the 'antiquated words, harsh expressions, grammatical inaccuracies, . . . awkward inversions, identical or otherwise faulty rhymes, and a literality carried so far as to make some passages look

more like versified prose than poetry'. But in the end
it became 'the decided conviction of the Committee
that, for the present at all events, the best expedient
[is] to retain the existing version without the slight-
est alteration, but to supplement it by duplicate translations; including in these such portions as one thought
most faulty in point of style'. That is to say, the idea
recommended by the Committee to the Assembly was
not any tampering with the existing text, but the
enlargement of the number of second versions, in other
metres than the common metre which, except in thirteen cases, dominates the whole version.

In a Report written by Dr. Neil Livingston, the
erudite editor of the great reprint of the 1635 Psalter,
the Committee used cogent arguments by which to
recommend their scheme.

One reason they urged for additional metres was

'furnished by the natural love of diversified poetic rhythm. It is
a law of man's constitution to take pleasure in such variety, and
of this the whole history of poetry, ancient and modern, teems
with illustrations. . . . If the use of metre is to be defended against
those who contend for the chanting of the Psalms in prose, it
does not place the argument on an advantageous basis to strip
it of that element of interest which variety affords. Nor is it
wise, in a service which at the best is very liable to be treated
with indifference, to have one of the instincts of human nature
traversed and trampled upon, instead of being employed to
enhance and enrich.'

Again:

'the satisfactory translation of the Psalms, in a literary point of
view, requires variety of external form. Though it is a doubtful
question whether Hebrew poetry originally involved any

metrical structure, it seems to be generally admitted that, rhythmically at least, it is largely diversified. But a more obvious consideration consists in the range of subjects which the Psalms embrace, such as the didactic, the eucharistic, the penitential, the precatory, the historical, the descriptive; and in the extensive field of religious emotions over which they expatiate—the sorrowful, the pathetic, the solemn, the placid, the cheerful, the triumphant. What poet would admit that all of these should be run into the same mould? . . . Various recent translators are so much impressed with this consideration, that when the longer psalms exhibit strong changes of sentiment, they throw the various portions into diverse forms of metrical structure.

'Musical considerations [the argument continues] run strongly in the same direction. The rhythmic feeling is exercised in music as well as in poetry, and when both combine, the power of the alternations of strong and weak pulses is more impressively perceived, and the pleasure afforded by variety decidedly increased. Again, through paucity of metre, large accumulations of superior music are practically useless. The chorales of Germany, the fatherland of Church song, are shut out from the domain of [Scottish] worship except by a process of adaptation, which might, in most cases, be better termed laceration. [Various tunes] of first-class excellence, contained in the Reformation Psalters, are now nonentities to Scotland, because there is nothing to sing them to.'

It is impossible not to feel the force of these arguments; and it must have been felt very much more by the people of 1866, for they had no refuge such as we have, in hymns, from the monotony of unvarying common metre.

The Free Church Committee supported their excellent arguments by twenty-six examples of Psalms in various metres, which they recommended, and eighteen others to which attention was directed. Their proposal at that time did not convince the Assembly: but this was the first step towards the publication in 1873 of *Psalm-Versions, Paraphrases and Hymns,* and that in its turn led on to the *Free Church Hymnbook* of 1882.

Since that time no serious attempt has been made to revise or modify the traditional version, to remove the marks of its age, or to adapt its phraseology to the frequently too exigent requirements of modern taste or style. The Irish Presbyterian Church indeed did produce a version designed to obviate the awkward-nesses of phraseology and versification natural in the mid-seventeenth century, but now out of accord with present-day usages. But it is enough to say that their example has not been followed, and that most who have considered their handiwork have liked it so little that they would infinitely rather retain the version they know than sanction any similar irritating tinkering with it. The very stamp of age which the 1650 version wears is to many an attraction, and such minor diffi-culties as it usually presents are easy to overcome.

Not the least of its merits is one not often considered, but that is indicated on the title-page. 'The Psalms of David in metre, more plain, smooth, and agreeable to the Text than any heretofore.' The compilers were not aiming primarily at an agreeable poetical version such as would satisfy literary critics. Agreement with the text and plainness were the primary requisites. Smooth-ness was only a matter of taste, and if they could not in every case combine that with the other two require-ments, they had no hesitation in sacrificing smoothness to preserve them.

Q

Critics of weight have been found to praise these psalms because of the suitability of their style to the purpose they were meant to serve, and to regard their very lack of the smoother graces as a count in their favour. So eminent an Old Testament authority as Professor Robertson Smith held that

'as the Old Testament Church left for our guidance a perfect model of a childlike faith and devotion . . . it is essential that this model should be kept in all its simplicity. Every artificial touch, every trace of modern taste must be avoided. . . . A translation of the psalms for devotional use must be, above all things, simple, even naïve. This great requisite our Scottish version has fully realised, and to have done so is a merit that outweighs a hundred faults.'[1]

[1] Address in Aberdeen Free Church College, published in the *Presbyterian Psalmodist* for 1872, p. 105.

Chapter 20

The Future of Scottish Psalmody

FOR one reason or another, it must be admitted, long passages of the metrical Psalter are not suitable for present-day worship. In the original some of the Psalms were never intended to be sung. They were given their place in the Liturgy of the Second Temple, of which the Book of Psalms consists, to serve the purposes of personal and private devotion. Some are so steeped in Judaic imagery that they are quite alien to modern ideas. The sentiment of others is such as to impose silence on Christian lips: no power on earth can Christianize them. Their theology and ethic alike have been out-dated by the Christian revelation, and it is impossible to sing them without ignoring the teaching of Christ. For religious or moral reasons, therefore, there must be selection in our use of them, whether they be sung in verse or in prose.

In many cases, also, the versification in the metrical version is too rough and crude to furnish a natural or easy language for present-day devotion. Yet many passages which are intolerable in metre become practicable in prose. One foresees, therefore, in the course of time, a partial reversion to the primitive practice of chanting the prose version, to enlarge the number of Psalms which we can, with entirely consenting minds, incorporate in our worship. But the day when chanting in prose will be generally acceptable in most Scottish churches is still far away.

And for Scots folk, honourably tenacious as they are of long tradition, no substitute will ever take the place of the metrical psalms. It is true that the centuries-long contention between musicians and people of which this book is the story, has come at last to a point at which both sides may be reasonably satisfied with the share accorded them in the Church's services. The main part of what is sung in the common worship belongs to the people; so far the demand of the Reformers and their successors has been fully conceded. But the musicians also have vindicated the claims of their art to high honour in the materials and the mode in which music bears its part. Choirs are universal, and the standard of their singing sets a standard for the people. The organ, which has been called 'the instrument of God' because of its pre-eminent suitability for use in Divine worship, has received wide acceptance, and the organist is given recognition as the minister's coadjutor in the worthy ordering of the musical part of the service. Welcome has long since been given to the rich addition to the Church's materials of praise brought by the resources of Christian hymnody. Most people are aware that in the anthem the Word of God is being sung to them, as from lectern and pulpit it is read and preached. But notwithstanding all these gains it will be long before anything can take the place of a metrical Psalm with the great mass of ordinary church people, as the most authentic voice of their own praise. In the portions of the Psalter suitable for modern worship there is a rugged strength, a massive positiveness, an elevation and dignity and a direct objectivity, which make them incomparable for congregational use. And when we reflect that they have been interwoven with our national history for full three hundred years, and for a long period of that time have furnished our people with the only medium of their praise, we are poor Scotsmen if we do not feel that they have a special title to reverent honour as part of our religious heritage.

Already there are signs that that honour is diminishing. It is not an unusual experience to share in a service in which no place is given for one of the national Psalms. It is not the verdict of conservatism only, that psychologically and religiously that is a mistake. There are many people still who feel that they have been deprived of something to which their history gives them a right, and have been made unwilling partners in the surrender of a precious part of their heritage, when in their corporate worship they are given no chance of singing, even once, what more than anything unites them with their fellow worshippers in a song of praise to God in which the skilled and the unskilled, the cultured and the common people—all, equally—can join.

There is no excuse in the alleged narrow range of portions that all can sing. At the end of the Metrical Psalter there is a list of over a hundred passages which are perfectly suitable for use; but the choice among them tends to be shamefully narrow, and it is narrowed further still by the wholly erroneous idea that the first act of public worship must necessarily be a metrical Psalm. Many portions are more fittingly in place in the middle of the service, as, for instance, between the Lessons; others can nowhere be better used than in bringing the service to a close.

It is not improbable that when a revision of the *Church Hymnary* next takes place, a section of it will be devoted to a selection of the best metrical Psalms. This has been done in other Churches of the Presbyterian order, and the consequence has been that when the selection of suitable passages has been presented visually within convenient compass, more varied use has been made of these rich materials of praise. There is no point in continuing to print, for mere custom's sake, so much which everyone knows will never be sung, and the argument for salving those portions that are still usable is irresistible.

But whatever course be taken, the Tercentenary of this historic Psalter should recall the whole Scottish Church to a reconsideration of its value—as a precious part of the national religious inheritance and as an incomparable medium of the national Church's praise. It should awaken in all thoughtful people who are sensitive to tradition, and alive to historical as well as religious values, a pride which will induce them, with zealous vigilance and care, to preserve as far as possible in the Church's use this venerable instrument of their country's worship.

INDEX

Marckant, John, 41, 49.
Marlorat, Augustin, 53.
Marot, Clément, 11–14, 16–17, 28.
Marot–Beza Psalter (1562), 18–19, 25, 27.
Mass, the, xii, xiii, xvii, xviii.
Melville, Andrew, 167.
— James, 52, 60, 130.
Menstrie Psalms, The, 86.
Metrical Psalmody, Why? xii.
Millar, Edward, 63–5, 69, 72–3.
Milman, Dean, 215, 218.
Missal, The, xii, 57.
Moderates, The, 170, 181, 212.
Modes, Ecclesiastical, 19–20, 39–40, 70–1, 75, 111.
Montgomerie, Alexander, 83.
Montgomery, James, 215, 218.
Monymusk Papers, 150.
Moore, Thomas, 162.
Moray, Regent, 57.
Mure of Rowallan, Sir William, 83, 93, 98, 102–3.

National Psalmody, The 201.
Nevay, John, 97.
Northern Psalter, The, 201.
Norton, Thomas, 40–1, 49.

Old Scottish Psalm Tunes, 188.
Order of Geneva, see *Book of Common Order.*

Paisley Abbey, R. A. Smith as Precentor at, 193.
— — Harmonic Choir, 193.
Paisley Abbey Congregational Psalmody, 194.
Palestrina, xx.
Panmure Papers, 61.
Paraphrases, The, 151, 211–19.
Peebles, David, 57–9.
Plainsong (-chant), xiii–xv, 75, 110, 122, 180.
Playford's *Divine Companion,* 180.
Polyphony, xvi–vii, xx, 70, 110, 146.
Pont, Robert, 46, 49, 82.

Practice-verses, 123, 151, 164–78.
Precentors, The Early, 126.
Precentors, The Great, 190.
Prick-song, 127.
Pritchard, T. C. L., 205.
Proper Tunes, 65.
Psalms of David in Meeter, 211.
Psalm-Singer's Divine Companion, 162.
Psalters: see Aberdeen, Anglo-Genevan, Bay, English, French, Irish, Lausanne, Marot–Beza, Rous, St. Andrews, Scottish, Sternhold and Hopkins, Strasburg, Tate and Brady, Wedderburn.
Pullain, John, 31–2, 36, 49.

Quire Offices, xii, xiii.

Raban, Edward, 55, 68.
Ramsay, Allan, 118, 134, 177.
Reformation Psalter, see Scottish Psalter of, 1564.
Reports, Tunes in, 55, 66, 68, 70–1, 121, 186.
Revolution Settlement, 118, 131.
Rous, Francis, 79, 90–3, 97, 100–4.
Row, John, 97.
Rowallan Lute Book, 83.
Roxburghe Ballads, 167.
Rudiments of Music, 139, 169, 191.
Run-line, The, see 'Lining'.

Sacred Harmony of the Church of Scotland, 195.
Sacred Music Institution (Glasgow), 201.
St. Andrews Music Manuscript, A, 137.
— Psalter, 56–63, 65, 72.
St. Cecilia's Hall, 118, 140, 202.
Scone Antiphonary, xvi.
Scott, Sir Walter, 142, 213–14, 216–18.
Scottish Collects of 1595, 53–4.
Scottish Psalter of 1564: 15, 31–2,

PRINTED IN
GREAT BRITAIN
AT THE
UNIVERSITY PRESS
OXFORD
BY
CHARLES BATEY
PRINTER
TO THE
UNIVERSITY